THE NEW CLARENDON SHAKESPEARE

Under the general editorship of
R. E. C. HOUGHTON, M.A.
Fellow and Tutor of St. Peter's Hall
Lecturer in English Literature, Oriel College, Oxford

Edited by

As You Like It	ISABEL J. BISSON, M.A., formerly Lecturer in English in the University of Birmingham.
Hamlet	GEORGE RYLANDS, Fellow of King's College, Cambridge.
Henry IV, Part II	WILLIAM R. RUTLAND, B.A., B. LITT., D. PHIL., formerly Noble Research Fellow in English in the University of Liverpool.
Henry V	R. F. W. FLETCHER, M.A., Fellow and Senior Tutor of St. Edmund Hall, Oxford.
Julius Caesar	R. E. C. HOUGHTON.
Macbeth	BERNARD GROOM, M.A., formerly Senior English Master of Clifton College.
Merchant of Venice	R. F. W. FLETCHER.
Midsummer Night's Dream	F. C. HORWOOD, M.A., Tutor of St. Catherine's Society, Oxford.
Richard II	J. M. LOTHIAN, M.A., Professor of English in the University of Saskatchewan.
Romeo and Juliet	R. E. C. HOUGHTON.
The Tempest	J. R. SUTHERLAND, M.A., B.LITT., Professor of English at Queen Mary College, London.
Twelfth Night	J. C. DENT, M.A., Headmaster of Westminster City School, London.

12/50.

THE NEW CLARENDON SHAKESPEARE

THE
TEMPEST

Edited by

J. R. SUTHERLAND

Professor of English Literature
in the University of London

OXFORD
AT THE CLARENDON PRESS

Oxford University Press, Amen House, London E.C. 4

GLASGOW NEW YORK TORONTO MELBOURNE WELLINGTON
BOMBAY CALCUTTA MADRAS CAPE TOWN

Geoffrey Cumberlege, Publisher to the University

FIRST PUBLISHED 1939
REPRINTED 1941, 1947, 1950

PRINTED IN GREAT BRITAIN
AT THE UNIVERSITY PRESS, OXFORD
BY CHARLES BATEY, PRINTER TO THE UNIVERSITY

GENERAL PREFACE

This edition of Shakespeare aims primarily at presenting the text in such a way that it can be easily read and understood. The language of Shakespeare presents considerable difficulties to the beginner, difficulties which are soon forgotten and overlooked by readers who are familiar with the plays. The answers of examination candidates often reveal unexpected ignorance of quite ordinary Shakespearian phraseology and vocabulary. In the notes, therefore, the main emphasis has been placed on the interpretation of words and phrases. Textual and linguistic matter, to which much space was given in the old Clarendon Press editions of Wright and Clark, has been kept in the background, but explanation is prominent. The notes have been divided; words and phrases capable of a short explanation are glossed at the foot of the page, while the more difficult passages are treated after the text in the general commentary.

In the commentary alternative explanations and the mention of critics by name have been avoided as far as possible; on the other hand there are a number of less elementary notes on textual points and other matters not strictly necessary for younger students, and these appear in smaller type and within square brackets.

After the commentary is printed a substantial selection from the best criticism of the play, old and new; a feature in which this edition of Shakespeare follows the plan set by the Clarendon English Series. Here some matter will be found suitable for more advanced students; and the inclusion of varying opinions will provide material for reflection and comparison. It is the editor's belief that students can best be taught to criticize by the provision of material which they may use as a starting-point as well as a model.

ACKNOWLEDGEMENTS

THE editor would like to acknowledge his debt to the *Oxford English Dictionary*, to the Arden edition of *The Tempest* by M. Luce for a number of valuable suggestions, and to the general editor of this series.

The editor also gratefully thanks the following for permission to reprint passages from copyright works: Sir Edmund Chambers and Messrs. Blackie & Son Ltd. (Preface to *The Tempest* from *The Red Letter Shakespeare*); Western Reserve University, Cleveland, Ohio (A. H. Thorndike, *The Influence of Beaumont and Fletcher on Shakespeare*); The Macmillan Company, New York (W. W. Lawrence, *Shakespeare's Problem Comedies*); The Syndics of the Cambridge University Press (Sir A. T. Quiller-Couch, *Shakespeare's Workmanship*); Mr. R. Noble and the Oxford University Press (*Shakespeare's Use of Song*); Dr. J. W. Mackail (*The Approach to Shakespeare*); Messrs. George G. Harrap & Co. Ltd. (L. L. Schücking, *Character Problems in Shakespeare*); The Modern Language Association of America (E. E. Stoll, *The Tempest*; from *P.M.L.A.* xlvii); The Executor of the late Lytton Strachey, Messrs. Chatto & Windus, and Messrs. Harcourt, Brace & Co. Ltd. (Lytton Strachey, *Books and Characters*); The Executors of the late John Bailey and Messrs. Longmans Green & Co. Ltd. (John Bailey, *Shakespeare*); The Harvard University Press (G. L. Kittredge, *Shakespeare*).

The text of The Tempest *here printed is complete except for one phrase.*

CONTENTS

CONTENTS

INTRODUCTION
DATE

When, in 1623, John Heminge and Henry Condell collected and published the plays of their fellow actor, Shakespeare, they placed *The Tempest* at the beginning of the volume. But no one believes that it was an early play. It was certainly one of the last—possibly the very last—to be written; and the reason for placing it first in the Folio may have been the very fact that it was still fresh in the memory of the public. It was probably acted for the first time in 1611. Apart from the fact that it has all the marks of Shakespeare's latest style, and has a good deal in common with three of his latest plays, *Pericles*, *Cymbeline*, and *The Winter's Tale* [see Select Literary Criticism, 'The Style of *The Tempest*' and 'Shakespeare's Last Plays'], there are some more particular reasons for fixing the date fairly confidently about the year 1611.

(*a*) The earliest mention of the play occurs in the Account Books of the Revels Office. 'A play called the Tempest' was acted before James I on Hallowmass night (i.e. November 1), 1611. It was acted again during the winter of 1612–13, as part of the celebrations at Court in honour of the betrothal of the Princess Elizabeth, daughter of King James I, with Frederick, the Prince Palatine Elector.

(*b*) In the summer of 1609 a fleet of ships bound for Virginia encountered a hurricane off the West Indies, and the flagship of Sir George Somers, the *Sea-Venture*, was driven ashore upon the coast of the Bermudas (the 'vexed Bermoothes' of the play). The vessel was wrecked, being blown 'between two rockes, where she was fast lodged and locked'; but the crew made a fortunate escape. The rest of the fleet, as in *The Tempest*, escaped destruction. By May of the following year (1610) the shipwrecked mariners had built themselves two boats out of the cedar trees growing on the island, and in these they managed to reach Virginia. From there the news of their adventures was carried to England. Various accounts of the disaster were in print by 1610, and Shakespeare was clearly indebted to some of these when writing his play. *The Tempest*, therefore, cannot be earlier than 1610, unless there already existed some earlier version which did not make use of these accounts.

(*c*) The Masque in Act IV, scene i, which is generally accepted as having been written for some particular wedding in high life, would be an invaluable aid to dating the play if we could be quite sure whose wedding it was intended for originally. In view of the fact that the play was presented at Court as part of the festivities for the royal wedding of 1613, there are strong grounds for supposing that the masque was written especially for the Princess Elizabeth and her bridegroom. But even if it could be proved that the masque was written for the King's daughter, and was not just repeated for her benefit from a previous performance, we should have dated the masque, but not the play itself. *The Tempest*, in fact, may have been, and probably was, revised for performance at Court, and if so, the play that we now have is almost certainly that revision, and not the original play.

There can be no doubt, however, that the play was written in the closing period of Shakespeare's career, by a dramatist approaching his fiftieth year, and mature in his experience both of life and play-writing.

SOURCES OF THE PLAY

The idea of writing a play in which a vessel was cast away on a remote island may well have come to Shakespeare from the accounts of the 1609 shipwreck already mentioned. Before, or during, composition he certainly made some use of Silvester Jourdan's *A Discovery of the Barmudas, otherwise called the Ile of Divels* (1610). Jourdan was one of the survivors of the wreck, and his brief pamphlet describes the storm and gives some account of the island. A rather puzzling source is William Strachey's *A true reportory of the wracke and redemption of Sir Thomas Gates, Knight,* dated July 15, 1610, but not published, as far as we know, until some years after Shakespeare's death. (Gates shared the command of the expedition with Sir George Somers.) There are a number of verbal parallels in Strachey's narrative so striking as to make it almost certain that Shakespeare had read it—presumably in manuscript. Extracts from both of these accounts are given in Appendix IV. He may also have read and made use of one or two contemporary sources, such as Robert Rich's ballad, *Newes from Virginia,* but these are of minor importance.

The actual shipwreck, however important to the play, occupies only a small part of the action. Did Shakespeare simply invent the main theme of the banished duke-turned-magician who revenges himself benevolently upon his enemies ? Here, too, a source has been suggested. There are a number of noticeable resemblances between the situation in *The Tempest* and that in a German play, *Die Schöne Sidea* ('The Fair Sidea'), by Jacob Ayrer of Nuremberg, who died in 1605. In the latter play there is no desert island and there is no storm; but there is a prince who practises magic, and who is attended by a familiar spirit. He, too, has a lovely daughter, and she falls in love with the son of her father's greatest enemy. These are perhaps the commonplaces of romance, but there are a few resemblances on points of detail which have rather more significance. The young man, for instance, is prevented from drawing his sword by the prince's magic, and he is forced to carry logs in the same circumstances as Shakespeare's Ferdinand. But is it likely that Shakespeare had ever heard of *Die Schöne Sidea*? It is not, at any rate, impossible. A company of English players had visited Nuremberg in 1604, and they may have seen the play performed and brought back some account of it. On the other hand, the resemblances between the two plays, if they are not just coincidences, may be due to the fact that both Ayrer and Shakespeare were working on a common source; and that source, if it existed, is unknown to us.

THE PLACE OF THE PLAY IN CONTEMPORARY DRAMA

The Tempest inevitably invites comparison with that much earlier fairy play of Shakespeare's, *A Midsummer Night's Dream* (1595?); but it has more in common with two plays written late in his dramatic career, *Cymbeline* and *The Winter's Tale*, and with yet another in which he certainly had a hand, *Pericles*. Too much may have been made of the serenity of those late plays, but they are all alike at least in being romantic in tone. They abound in improbable and unexpected events: an old man is eaten by a bear, a baby princess is brought up among shepherds. Characters act in an arbitrary fashion, and character study is of less interest to the dramatist than incident or the incidental charms of poetry, music, song, and dance. After much misunderstanding and suffering these plays end in reconciliation and peace; there is plenty of cloud in the sky, but the sun breaks through at the end of the day. The parents have known tragedy, but their children restore their lost happiness. These last plays do, in fact, form a distinctive group in Shakespeare's dramatic output, and they seem to represent an effort on his part to comply with the changing tastes of the public.

Since the accession of James I in 1603, the connexion between Court and Theatre had become much closer, and as a result the Court was beginning to impose its tastes on

the stage. The dramatists who understood and met the
new demand most completely were Francis Beaumont and
John Fletcher. Writing in collaboration, those two were
producing a succession of lively dramatic entertainments,
witty, poetical, stimulating, but demanding no greater
effort of concentration than a fashionable audience is
normally disposed to make. A romantic play like their
Philaster (1610) is packed with incident, violent and
arbitrary characters, unexpected reversals of fortune, sur-
prises of every description. There is abundance of wit,
pathos, and pretty sentiment, and after astonishing vicis-
situdes all comes right in the end. A dogged individualist
like Ben Jonson might despise this sort of thing, and might
persist in giving the public what he wanted, and not what
they were asking for; but Shakespeare moved with his
times if he could not make the times move with him. It is
therefore reasonable to suppose that the romantic plays of
his closing years, differing in some ways from anything he
had previously written, were his response to the changing
demands of the Jacobean audiences.

In one important respect, at any rate, the Court taste
was undoubtedly making itself felt in these last plays. One
of the favourite diversions of James I and his court was the
Masque. This entertainment was traditionally based on
some subject from pagan mythology, but the 'book', or
libretto, was the least important part of it. The significant
features were song, dance, music, and spectacle; the
scenery and 'machines' were often elaborate and ingenious,
and the costumes were costly and splendid. From being
the diversion of the court, performed by the courtiers themselves, the masque spread to the professional stage. It is,
therefore, not without significance that in *Cymbeline*, *The
Winter's Tale*, and *Pericles*, masque elements are present,
and that they are to be found, still more notably, in *The
Tempest*.

THE SUPERNATURAL ELEMENT IN THE PLAY

How far belief in witches, fairies, and other supernatural agencies had begun to wane since Shakespeare was a young man it would be hard to say. Marlowe's *Dr. Faustus* and Greene's *Friar Bacon and Friar Bungay* are interesting examples of plays which treated a supernatural theme some twenty years before *The Tempest* was written. No doubt scepticism was increasing, though women suspected of witchcraft continued to be burnt in England for a hundred years after Shakespeare's death. But the coming of James I to London undoubtedly stimulated popular interest in magic and the occult; for James took a great interest in the supernatural, and was himself the author of a treatise on the subject, *Daemonologie*, published in 1597. It may be that in Prospero and his magic we have a dramatic study undertaken with at least one eye on the known interests of the learned Scottish king.

Elizabethan and Jacobean ideas about magic are confusing. At one time it seems as if all magic was regarded as wicked, at another time there appears to be a clear-cut distinction between black and white magic. Prospero, at any rate, is a benevolent magician; he has not entered into any compact with the devil, he has not sold his soul to the Evil One, like Dr. Faustus, but has acquired his power over the spirit world by hard study—by what to-day we should probably call 'research'.

'Prospero may be compared with Faustus, if only for the sake of contrasting the two types of magician, the good and the bad. Faustus and Prospero both have the Renaissance love of learning, but Faustus studies magic because it is forbidden knowledge, Prospero because it is philosophical research. Faustus sells his soul to gratify his senses; Prospero's magic is "not damnable", and he only uses it to work his deliverance from evil men. The magic that Faustus studies is the black art, diabolic and execrable; Prospero's "art" is not malignant, not even "mischievously good", like that of "white witches"; it is simply the acquisition of extraordinary powers, by means of astronomy and of cabalistic studies. It is an art external to himself, depending on calculations and spells, and on magic paraphernalia, book, wand, and mantle; without these he is powerless. His soul is clear of all dealings with the evil one. . . . When he breaks his wand and buries his book, he is merely the learned prince.' (H. Littledale, in *Shakespeare's England*, vol. i, pp. 541–2.)

It is significant, indeed, that at the close of the play Prospero should formally abjure his magic. Greene's Friar Bacon had done so too, and just as solemnly. When Prospero tells us in Act V,

> I'll break my staff,
> Bury it certain fathoms in the earth,
> And, deeper than did ever plummet sound,
> I'll drown my book,

he is acknowledging the danger, even in his hands, of the semi-illicit studies he has been pursuing, and reassuring the more nervous among his audience that from now on he will have no dealings with the forbidden world of spirits.

THE TEXT OF THE PLAY

The Tempest was first printed in 1623 in the collected edition of Shakespeare's plays known as the First Folio.

To the ordinary reader the interpretation of certain passages in the play will probably present some difficulty, but he will usually be inclined to blame himself for his lack of understanding. If he is also tempted at times to fix some of the blame on Shakespeare, it will be on account of his hurried and packed writing; it will scarcely occur to him that the play he is reading has been hastily revised, or is a drastically altered version of some earlier drama on the same subject. To the eye of the scholar, however—or, rather, of some scholars—there appear to be good reasons for suspecting that *The Tempest* as we now have it differs considerably from the play as Shakespeare originally wrote it. The whole question is highly controversial, and the evidence offered is occasionally too technical to be dealt with here; but the following are some of the main arguments in favour of the view that the play was abridged some time after its first production, by Shakespeare himself or by some other hand.

(*a*) There are a number of loose ends and discrepancies, awkward transitions, and incomplete lines of blank verse, all suggesting cuts in the text. Antonio, for instance, is said to have had a son in the wrecked vessel (I. ii. 434–5), but he never appears with the other gentlemen. Had he a small part in some earlier version? Francisco appears on several occasions, and is allotted a speech of ten lines in Act II, scene i, but apart from that he speaks only three more words in the play (III. iii. 40). Was his part drastically cut when (and if) the play was revised? Trinculo is described in the dramatis personae as 'a Jester', and he apparently wears the motley; but there are few indications in the text that he is a professional clown. What has happened to his quips?

(*b*) The same characters in the same scene sometimes talk in verse, sometimes in prose. This is not without parallel in Shakespeare, but it is unusual, and is regarded by some scholars as a clear indication of hasty revision.

(*c*) Act I, scene ii—by far the longest scene in the play— is almost wholly devoted to a description of events that have taken place off stage, some of them many years before the action of the play commences. Few Elizabethan plays are without a certain amount of this retrospective narrative, but the extent to which it is carried in *The Tempest* is quite exceptional. It has therefore been suggested that in its original form *The Tempest* was a play constructed like *The Winter's Tale* or *Pericles*, in which the action was spread out over a long period of years, and the various events were almost all shown—not described—on the stage. According to this view, *The Tempest* would probably have begun with the banishment of Prospero, and we should have seen Miranda as an infant. No reputable critic denies that the long exposition in Act I, scene ii, is the work of Shakespeare, and of Shakespeare exerting his full powers; but some, at least, prefer to regard it as a great *tour de force*, thrust upon the dramatist by the need to reduce an earlier play to make room for new matter.

(*d*) This 'new matter', it has been suggested, consists of the masque in Act IV. (Even *with* the masque, which could be lifted out of the play without much loss to the dramatic structure, *The Tempest* is the shortest but one of Shakespeare's plays.) A drama in which a noble Duke is seen giving the hand of his only daughter to a handsome young Prince was obviously peculiarly fitted to grace the royal wedding ceremonies of 1613; it would be still more fitting if the author were to include a masque specially written for the royal lovers. This, it is suggested again, is just what Shakespeare did; and to make room for the masque, and also to avoid wearying the noble guests with too lengthy an entertainment, he abridged his own play, which had previously been presented on the public stage. And finally, when Heminge and Condell came to publish *The Tempest* with the rest of Shakespeare's plays, it was this shortened *ad hoc* version that they handed to the printer.

Admittedly, this is for the most part ingenious guess-work; we do not *know* that these things happened. Most of the arguments offered in favour of this theory of revision and abridgement have been adequately met, and the evidence on which they are based either questioned or differently interpreted. What is new and plausible is not necessarily true. Certainly, too, the revision theory would be doing a great deal of mischief if it induced readers of this play to think that they were reading a carelessly botched play, hurriedly adapted for a particular occasion, and then as rapidly stuffed again with matter of local and temporary interest. That is not the impression that it has given to generations of readers and playgoers. Whatever happened to *The Tempest*—and whether anything happened at all except that Shakespeare wrote it and his company played it—it is in its compactness, its freshness, its bold contrasts of character, its imagination, its masterly treatment of the supernatural, its poetry, and its spectacular appeal, one of the most memorable of his plays.

[The arguments for one or more revisions of *The Tempest* are to be found in the first volume of the new edition of Shakespeare, edited by A. Quiller-Couch and J. Dover Wilson, and published by the Cambridge University Press in 1921. A reply to most of these arguments was published in *The Review of English Studies*, vol. i (1925), by E. K. Chambers.]

This edition follows the text of the *Oxford Shakespeare*, except that the Folio is restored in I. ii. 146, 327, 330, 384, 460, 485; II. i. 122, 130, 160, 176; II. ii. 57, 62; III. i. 15; III. ii. 148–9; IV. i. 3; V. i. 39, 117, 230. The Folio stage directions have been restored at III. iii. 17, 82; and IV. i. 102, 164.

THE PLOT OF THE PLAY

I. i. *The Tempest* opens with a noisy scene on board ship. A storm is driving the ship ashore in spite of the mariners' efforts to head her out to sea. Alonso, Sebastian, Antonio, Ferdinand, and Gonzalo all appear on deck. The scene closes with the foundering of the vessel.

I. ii. This scene (in length about a quarter of the play)

falls into four sections. From ll. 1 to 186 Prospero and
Miranda are alone upon the stage, while Prospero gives his
daughter an account of his past life in Milan. Miranda is
then charmed to sleep by her father (189). Prospero now
summons Ariel, his familiar spirit, and Ariel reports how
he has harassed all on board the ship at Prospero's bidding,
and left the ship safe at anchor with the mariners asleep
under hatches. Alonso and the rest he has brought safe
ashore, and 'dispers'd them 'bout the isle'. Ariel thinks
that he has now done enough for his master, but Prospero
reminds Ariel of how he gave him his liberty, and threatens
to take it away again if he proves mutinous. Ariel vanishes
promptly to do Prospero's bidding (187–304). Prospero
wakens Miranda, and together they go to visit Caliban, the
son of a witch, Sycorax, whom Prospero found living on
the island when he landed there. Caliban comes out of his
den, and curses Prospero, who orders him to fetch firewood,
and threatens him with aches and pains if he refuses.
Caliban goes out grumbling (305–74). Ariel reappears,
playing and singing. He is followed by the King's son,
Ferdinand, who is convinced that he is the sole survivor
from the wreck. Miranda catches sight of him, the first
young man she has ever set eyes upon, and is lost in
admiration. The two converse eagerly, to the delight of
Prospero, who has brought them together in the hope that
they may fall in love, but he conceals his feelings for the
present, and speaks sternly to Ferdinand. Ferdinand
attempts to draw his sword, but is prevented by Prospero's
magic, and is led away a prisoner (375–498).

II. i. In another part of the island Alonso is mourning
for the supposed loss of his son. Gonzalo tries to comfort
him; Antonio and Sebastian joke heartlessly. Ariel
appears, and charms Alonso and Gonzalo and the other
lords to sleep; only Antonio and Sebastian are left awake.
Antonio suggests a brutal plot to murder the sleeping King.

He has just persuaded Sebastian to fall upon the sleeping
Gonzalo while he himself dispatches Alonso, when Ariel
reappears 'invisible', and wakens the sleepers. For the
time, at least, Alonso is safe.

II. ii. Caliban bearing his logs meets with Trinculo, and,
believing him to be a spirit of Prospero's sent to torture
him, falls flat on his face. A storm blowing up, Trinculo
takes shelter under Caliban's cloak. The two are lying
together on the ground, when Stephano staggers in drunk
and singing. Stephano gives Caliban a drink from his
bottle. Caliban, taking him for a god, enters gladly into
his service.

III. i. A love scene between Ferdinand (who is now pil-
ing logs for Prospero) and Miranda. He declares his love for
Miranda. She tells him frankly, 'I am your wife if you will
marry me.' Prospero looks on approvingly from behind.

III. ii. Caliban, Stephano, and Trinculo are still drinking. Caliban now sees a chance of revenging himself on his
master, and tells Stephano that he can lead him to Prospero's cell, where Stephano can brain him while he sleeps,
and so become King of the island and marry Miranda.
Ariel, who has been listening all this time, leads the conspirators away by the sound of his tabor and pipe.

III. iii. Alonso and his company, tired out with searching for Ferdinand, hear a solemn music, and see several
strange shapes bearing in a banquet. Before they can
touch the food the banquet vanishes—another of Prospero's
magic tricks. Ariel convicts the 'three men of sin'. Alonso
rushes away distracted, followed by Antonio and Sebastian.
All three are under Prospero's spell.

IV. i. Prospero now formally gives his daughter to
Ferdinand, and entertains them with a masque, once again
the work of Ariel and his fellow spirits. Suddenly he
remembers Caliban and his confederates, who, as he knows,
are now on their way to murder him. Ariel has meanwhile

led them a sorry dance through thorns and briers, and finally plunged them in a filthy pool. They now enter, wet. Caliban is impatient to have Prospero killed, but Stephano and Trinculo waste their time stealing trifles which Prospero has made Ariel hang on a line outside his cell. Finally Prospero's spirits in the form of hounds hunt them about the stage, Prospero and Ariel 'setting them on'.

V. i. Prospero with his staff traces a magic circle on the ground. Alonso, &c., enter the circle, and stand charmed. Prospero is now free to talk to them at leisure, and he does so. He discloses who he is, and explains what has been happening during the last few hours. At length he draws the curtain that conceals his cell, and Ferdinand and Miranda are discovered playing chess together. Alonso and Prospero are reconciled by the loves of their children. Antonio and Sebastian are sternly forgiven, or, at least, left without further punishment. Caliban and his companions, thoroughly racked by Prospero's spirits, are dismissed with contempt, and Ariel—at last—is free. Next day the whole company will sail with Prospero to Naples, where the marriage of Ferdinand and Miranda will be duly solemnized.

THE PLAY ON THE SHAKESPEARIAN STAGE

The Elizabethan theatre was a very different affair from the modern one. The latter, a 'picture stage' in which the audience may be said to constitute the 'fourth wall' of a room, aims at illusion; the former, in which the stage was a platform thrust out among an audience, could not hope for this. A glance at the illustration will make a long explanation unnecessary. The platform constitutes the front or main stage; entrance was at the back (through any of several doors), not at the sides, so that some time elapsed between a character's appearance and his reaching the front of the stage. The building at the rear had a

gallery above, which served for walls of a city, balcony of
a room, &c. Below were curtains which, when drawn back,
served to provide a *rear* or *inner stage*. As there was no
means of closing the outer stage, scenes which had to be
disclosed or hidden took place on this inner stage. There
was little approximation to scenery, but plenty of movable
properties (e.g. a 'mossy bank').

Theatres in Shakespeare's day were either 'public' or
'private'. The public theatre, like the 'Fortune' on page 21,
was open to the sky, with the outer stage only partly roofed
over; the private theatre, though the stage still jutted into
the auditorium, was completely roofed over, and was, in
fact, an indoors theatre, lit by artificial light. Though called
'private', it was open to the public. In 1608 Shakespeare's
company acquired one of these private theatres, the 'Black-
friars', and it is possible that *The Tempest* was first performed there rather than in their public theatre, 'The
Globe'. Private theatres were more intimate, and were
better suited for the representation of a long quiet conversation such as that in Act I, scene ii, of *The Tempest*;
and they had also an advantage over public theatres in the
matter of scenery and mechanical devices. A play with so
many 'quaint devices' and vanishings, not to mention a
descent of Juno from above, could be more easily acted on
the stage of a private than of a public theatre.

In *The Tempest* the first scene probably took place on
the outer stage, but possibly on the inner, or even the
upper, stage; in either case there would be little but the
dialogue to indicate that the actors were supposed to be on
a ship at sea. The second scene would certainly be on the
outer stage; and the action remains there through the
whole of the second and third acts, except that in Act III,
scene iii, Prospero appears on the upper stage ('Prospero
on the top') and watches his spirits dancing in with the
banquet. In Act IV the action again takes place on the

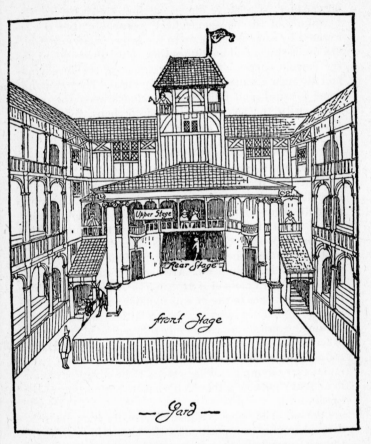

Upper Stage

Rear Stage

front Stage

— Yard —

THE FORTUNE THEATRE

A reconstruction by Mr. W. H. Godfrey from the builder's contract, which has survived.
The theatre was built in 1600, two years later than the Globe, at which most of
Shakespeare's plays were performed, and burnt down in 1621.

outer stage. The stage direction 'Juno descends' at the beginning of the masque indicates probably that she is lowered by some machine on to the stage. Act v opens on the outer stage, and continues there until Prospero draws the curtain concealing the inner stage, where Ferdinand and Miranda are discovered playing chess. They rise and come forward, and the action concludes upon the outer stage, with the actors passing off, perhaps, by way of Prospero's cell, i.e. the inner stage.

NOTE ON DRAMATIS PERSONAE

Ariel. The name of this delicate phantom—'thou which art but air', Prospero calls him—was almost certainly intended to convey the idea of 'an airy spirit'. The word actually occurs in Isaiah xxix. 1: 'Ariel, the city where David dwelt,' in the 'Bishop's Bible' of 1568 and in the Authorized Version of 1611, but had been 'used in magical writings for one of the spirits who control the elements or the planets' (E. K. Chambers). Ariel is reminiscent of Shakespeare's earlier fairies in *A Midsummer Night's Dream*, but he belongs rather to the race of familiar spirits or demons, who are summoned by a magician (as fairies are not) to do his bidding. Spirits were commonly differentiated from each other by the element in which they lived: earth, air, fire, water. Accordingly, one meets with gnomes, sylphs, salamanders, or nymphs. Ariel appears to be equally at home in all four elements, although his nature has nothing of the earth in it.

Caliban. The name 'Caliban' is usually thought to be derived from a transposition of the letters in 'Cannibal', though some hold that it comes from the gypsy word 'cauliban'='blackness'. The verb 'ban' in Shakespeare's day meant to 'curse', and as Caliban on his first appearance is heartily cursing Prospero, and continues to do so throughout the play, the idea of cursing may have been present in Shakespeare's mind when he invented the name. In spite of his origin, Caliban has not got superhuman powers; he is, rather, sub-human. But what does he look like? He is 'savage and deformed'. But is he, as Trinculo asks himself, 'a man or a fish'? According to Trinculo, he is 'legged like a man, and his fins like arms', and is 'half a fish, and half a monster'. Another witness, Antonio, declares quite independently that he is 'a plain fish'. On the other hand, Caliban himself talks of digging up pig-nuts with his long nails—which one would not expect to find on fins. Before we see Caliban at all Prospero has described him as 'a freckled whelp', and the moment before he makes his first entry Prospero has shouted 'thou tortoise!' at him, though 'tortoise' here is, no doubt, more abusive than descriptive. We may be reasonably sure, at any rate, that the original Caliban (whose 'make-up', after all, was almost certainly settled by Shakespeare himself) had something uncouth and deformed in his appearance, and that somehow or other—by the movement of his arms, or by some actual hint of deformity in them—he at least suggested a fish. It is true that we use the phrase 'a queer fish' without much precise significance, but the references to Caliban's fish-like appearance (and smell) in *The Tempest* are too definite and too frequent to be explained away. The modern producer is generally content to suggest his savage nature by giving him long shaggy hair, and dressing him in skins.

The names Alonso, Sebastian, Antonio, Ferdinand, and Gonzalo all occur in Eden's *History of Travaille* (1577). It was almost certainly there that Shakespeare found the name of Caliban's father, the god Setebos. Prospero and Stephano were characters in the first, or Italian, version of Ben Jonson's *Every Man in his Humour*. This play was acted in 1596, with Shakespeare (who was an actor as well as a dramatist) in the cast.

DRAMATIS PERSONAE

ALONSO, King of Naples.
SEBASTIAN, his Brother.
PROSPERO, the right Duke of Milan.
ANTONIO, his Brother, the usurping Duke of Milan.
FERDINAND, Son to the King of Naples.
GONZALO, an honest old Counsellor.
ADRIAN, } Lords.
FRANCISCO, }
CALIBAN, a savage and deformed Slave.
TRINCULO, a Jester.
STEPHANO, a drunken Butler.
Master of a Ship, Boatswain, Mariners.
MIRANDA, Daughter to Prospero.
ARIEL, an airy Spirit.
IRIS, }
CERES, }
JUNO, } presented by Spirits.
Nymphs, }
Reapers, }

Other Spirits attending on Prospero.

SCENE—*The Sea, with a Ship; afterwards an Island.*

THE TEMPEST

ACT I

Scene I. ON A SHIP AT SEA. A TEMPESTUOUS NOISE
OF THUNDER AND LIGHTNING HEARD.

Enter a Shipmaster *and a* Boatswain *severally.*

Master. Boatswain!

Boatswain. Here, master: what cheer?

Master. Good, speak to the mariners: fall to't yarely, or
we run ourselves aground: bestir, bestir.   [*Exit.* 4

Enter Mariners.

Boatswain. Heigh, my hearts! cheerly, cheerly, my hearts!
yare, yare! Take in the topsail. Tend to the master's
whistle.—Blow, till thou burst thy wind, if room enough!

Enter ALONSO, SEBASTIAN, ANTONIO FERDINAND,
GONZALO, *and others.*

Alonso. Good boatswain, have care. Where's the master?
Play the men.

Boatswain. I pray now, keep below.   10

Antonio. Where is the master, boson?

*Glossarial notes dealing with words and phrases, and paraphrases of
difficult passages, are given at the foot of the page where such seem
necessary to keep the sense running. Other notes are printed in the
commentary at the end. The sign [N] in the footnotes indicates that
a further note on the same line will be found in the commentary.*

3 **Good**: good sir (vocative) [*N*].   **yarely**: briskly.
5 **cheerly**: be cheerful, do your work heartily.   **my hearts**:
cf. my hearties.   6 **yare!**: quick!   **Tend**: attend to.   7 **if
room enough**: so long as we have sea-room. [*N*].   9 **Play the
men**: act like (brave) men. [*N*].

Boatswain. Do you not hear him? You mar our labour: keep your cabins: you do assist the storm.

Gonzalo. Nay, good, be patient.   14

Boatswain. When the sea is. Hence! What cares these roarers for the name of king? To cabin: silence! trouble us not.

Gonzalo. Good, yet remember whom thou hast aboard.

Boatswain. None that I more love than myself. You are a counsellor: if you can command these elements 20 to silence, and work the peace of the present, we will not hand a rope more; use your authority: if you cannot, give thanks you have lived so long, and make yourself ready in your cabin for the mischance of the hour, if it so hap.—Cheerly, good hearts!—Out of our way, I 25 say.   *[Exit.*

Gonzalo. I have great comfort from this fellow: methinks he hath no drowning mark upon him; his complexion is perfect gallows. Stand fast, good Fate, to his hanging! make the rope of his destiny our cable, for our 30 own doth little advantage! If he be not born to be hanged, our case is miserable.   *[Exeunt.*

Re-enter Boatswain.

Boatswain. Down with the topmast! yare! lower, lower! Bring her to try with main-course. [*A cry within.*] A plague upon this howling! they are louder than the weather, or our office.—   36

Re-enter SEBASTIAN, ANTONIO, *and* GONZALO.

Yet again? what do you here? Shall we give o'er, and drown? Have you a mind to sink?

18 **Good**: cf. l. 3.   22 **hand**: handle.   28 **complexion**: aspect. [*N*].   31 **advantage**: (verb) prove beneficial.   34 **Bring her to try with main-course**: bring the ship close into the wind with only the mainsail set ('try' = 'lie to', sail close to the wind).   **35 they**: the passengers below.   **36 office**: function, job. [*N*].

Sebastian. A pox o' your throat, you bawling, blas-
phemous, incharitable dog!   40

Boatswain. Work you, then.

Antonio. Hang, cur, hang! you whoreson, insolent
noisemaker, we are less afraid to be drowned than thou art.

Gonzalo. I'll warrant him for drowning; though the ship
were no stronger than a nutshell.   45

Boatswain. Lay her a-hold, a-hold! Set her two courses;
off to sea again; lay her off.

Enter Mariners, *wet.*

Mariners. All lost! to prayers, to prayers! all lost!
                                                  [*Exeunt.*

Boatswain. What, must our mouths be cold?

Gonzalo. The king and prince at prayers! let us assist
     them,   50
For our case is as theirs.

Sebastian.   I am out of patience.

Antonio. We are merely cheated of our lives by drunk-
     ards.—
This wide-chapp'd rascal,—would thou might'st lie
     drowning,
The washing of ten tides!

Gonzalo.   He'll be hang'd yet,
Though every drop of water swear against it,   55
And gape at wid'st to glut him.
     [*A confused noise within,—*'Mercy on us!'—

44 **I'll warrant . . . drowning**: I'll guarantee he won't drown.
46 **Lay her a-hold**: bring her into the wind.   **her two
courses**: i.e. the foresail and the mainsail. [*N*].   47 **lay her
off**: steer her away from the shore.   49 **must our mouths
be cold?**: must we be drowned? [*N*].   52 **merely**: absolutely.
53 **wide-chapped**: wide-jawed. [*N*].   54 **The washing . . .
tides**: till ten tides have washed over you. [*N*].   56 **glut**:
swallow greedily.

'We split, we split!'—'Farewell, my wife and children!'—
'Farewell, brother!'—'We split, we split, we split!'—]

Antonio. Let's all sink wi' the king. [*Exit.*

Sebastian. Let's take leave of him. [*Exit.* 60

Gonzalo. Now would I give a thousand furlongs of sea for
an acre of barren ground; long heath, brown furze, any
thing. The wills above be done! but I would fain die a dry
death. [*Exit.*

Scene II. The Island: before the Cell of Prospero.

Enter PROSPERO *and* MIRANDA.

Miranda. If by your art, my dearest father, you have
Put the wild waters in this roar, allay them.
The sky, it seems, would pour down stinking pitch,
But that the sea, mounting to th' welkin's cheek,
Dashes the fire out. O! I have suffer'd   5
With those that I saw suffer: a brave vessel,
Who had, no doubt, some noble creatures in her,
Dash'd all to pieces. O! the cry did knock
Against my very heart. Poor souls, they perish'd.
Had I been any god of power, I would   10
Have sunk the sea within the earth, or e'er
It should the good ship so have swallow'd and
The fraughting souls within her.

Prospero.   Be collected:
No more amazement. Tell your piteous heart
There's no harm done.

Miranda.   O, woe the day!

Prospero.   No harm. 15

62 **long heath:** heather. [*N*].   62–3 **any thing:** i.e. however
barren. [*N*].   4 **welkin's:** sky's.   6 **brave:** gallant.   11
or e'er: before.   13 **fraughting:** forming a freight, or cargo.
Be collected: compose yourself.   14 **piteous:** pitiful. [*N*].

I have done nothing but in care of thee,—
Of thee, my dear one! thee, my daughter!—who
Art ignorant of what thou art, nought knowing
Of whence I am: nor that I am more better
Than Prospero, master of a full poor cell,   20
And thy no greater father.

   Miranda.   More to know
Did never meddle with my thoughts.

   Prospero.   'Tis time
I should inform thee further. Lend thy hand,
And pluck my magic garment from me.—So:

                       [*Lays down his mantle.*
Lie there, my art.—Wipe thou thine eyes; have comfort.
The direful spectacle of the wrack, which touch'd   26
The very virtue of compassion in thee,
I have with such provision in mine art
So safely order'd, that there is no soul—
No, not so much perdition as an hair,   30
Betid to any creature in the vessel
Which thou heard'st cry, which thou saw'st sink. Sit down;
For thou must now know further.

   Miranda.   You have often
Begun to tell me what I am, but stopp'd,
And left me to a bootless inquisition,   35
Concluding, 'Stay; not yet.'

   Prospero.   The hour's now come,
The very minute bids thee ope thine ear;
Obey and be attentive. Canst thou remember
A time before we came unto this cell?

19 **nor that:** and not knowing that. [*N*].   20 **full:** very.   21
thy no greater father: nothing grander than your father, i.e. not
a Duke.   22 **meddle with:** mingle with, engage.   26 **wrack:**
wreck.   27 **virtue:** soul, essence.   28 **provision:** preparation beforehand.   29 **no soul:** no one (hurt). [*N*].   30 **perdition:** loss. [*N*].   31 **Betid:** happened.   35 **bootless
inquisition:** unavailing inquiry.

I do not think thou canst, for then thou wast not   40
Out three years old.

   Miranda.   Certainly, sir, I can.

   Prospero. By what? by any other house or person?
Of anything the image tell me, that
Hath kept with thy remembrance.

   Miranda.   'Tis far off;
And rather like a dream than an assurance   45
That my remembrance warrants. Had I not
Four or five women once that tended me?

   Prospero. Thou hadst, and more, Miranda. But how is it
That this lives in thy mind? What seest thou else
In the dark backward and abysm of time?   50
If thou remember'st aught ere thou cam'st here,
How thou cam'st here, thou may'st.

   Miranda.   But that I do not.

   Prospero. Twelve year since, Miranda, twelve year since,
Thy father was the Duke of Milan and
A prince of power.

   Miranda.   Sir, are not you my father?   55

   Prospero. Thy mother was a piece of virtue, and
She said thou wast my daughter; and thy father
Was Duke of Milan, and his only heir
A princess,—no worse issued.

   Miranda.   O, the heavens!
What foul play had we that we came from thence?   60
Or blessed was't we did?

   Prospero.   Both, both, my girl:
By foul play, as thou say'st, were we heav'd thence;
But blessedly holp hither.

    41 Out: fully.   **46 remembrance warrants:** memory can
vouch for.   **47 tended:** looked after (or, perhaps, 'attended',
i.e. waited upon as servants).   **56 piece:** example.   **59 issued:**
born.   **61 Or blessed . . . did?:** was it a blessing (in disguise)
that we did?   **62 heav'd:** removed, carried away.   **63 holp:**
helped.

Miranda.   O! my heart bleeds
To think o' the teen that I have turn'd you to,
Which is from my remembrance. Please you further.   65
   Prospero. My brother and thy uncle, call'd Antonio,—
I pray thee, mark me,—that a brother should
Be so perfidious!—he whom next thyself,
Of all the world I lov'd, and to him put
The manage of my state; as at that time,   70
Through all the signiories it was the first,
And Prospero the prime duke; being so reputed
In dignity, and for the liberal arts,
Without a parallel: those being all my study,
The government I cast upon my brother,   75
And to my state grew stranger, being transported
And rapt in secret studies. Thy false uncle—
Dost thou attend me?
   Miranda.   Sir, most heedfully.
   Prospero. Being once perfected how to grant suits,
How to deny them, who t'advance, and who   80
To trash for over-topping; new created
The creatures that were mine, I say, or chang'd 'em,
Or else new form'd 'em; having both the key
Of officer and office, set all hearts i' the state
To what tune pleas'd his ear; that now he was   85
The ivy which had hid my princely trunk,
And suck'd my verdure out on't.—Thou attend'st not.

---

64 teen: sorrow.   **65 from my remembrance:** beyond
my recollection.   **Please you further:** tell me more, please.
70 manage: control (of a horse), administration.   **71 signiories:** domains.   **71 it:** my state, i.e. Milan was the first
(chief) of all states (in Italy) and Prospero first among dukes. [*N*].
76 transported: carried away.   **79 Being once perfected:**
having once thoroughly learnt.   **81 To trash for over-topping:**
to check if he was going ahead of the rest. [*N*].   **82 creatures:**
dependants.   **85 that:** so that.   **87 verdure:** sap,
vigour.   **on't:** of it.

Miranda. O, good sir! I do.

Prospero.   I pray thee, mark me.
I, thus neglecting worldly ends, all dedicated
To closeness and the bettering of my mind   90
With that, which, but by being so retir'd,
O'erpriz'd all popular rate, in my false brother
Awak'd an evil nature; and my trust,
Like a good parent, did beget of him
A falsehood in its contrary as great   95
As my trust was; which had indeed no limit,
A confidence sans bound. He being thus lorded,
Not only with what my revenue yielded,
But what my power might else exact,—like one,
Who having into truth, by telling of it,   100
Made such a sinner of his memory,
To credit his own lie,—he did believe
He was indeed the duke; out o' the substitution,
And executing th' outward face of royalty,
With all prerogative:—Hence his ambition growing,—
Dost thou hear?

Miranda.   Your tale, sir, would cure deafness.   106

Prospero. To have no screen between this part he play'd
And him he play'd it for, he needs will be
Absolute Milan. Me, poor man,—my library
Was dukedom large enough: of temporal royalties   110
He thinks me now incapable; confederates,—

---

90 **closeness:** retirement, solitude.   91 **that:** i.e. study.
but by . . . retir'd: but for the fact that it involves so much with-
drawal from public affairs.   92 **O'erpriz'd all popular rate:**
was worth more than the esteem of the people (i.e. popularity).
94 **of him:** in him. [*N*].   97 **sans:** without. **lorded:** ennobled.
99 **what . . . else:** (with) whatever else my power might.   102
To: as to. [*N*].   103 **out o' the substitution:** in consequence of
having taken my place.   109 **Absolute Milan:** the actual Duke
of Milan (but in l. 115, the city). [*N*].   110 **temporal royalties:**
worldly kingdom.   111 **confederates:** makes a bargain.

So dry he was for sway,—wi' the king of Naples
To give him annual tribute, do him homage;
Subject his coronet to his crown, and bend
The dukedom, yet unbow'd,—alas, poor Milan!—   115
To most ignoble stooping.
   Miranda.   O the heavens!
   Prospero. Mark his condition and the event; then tell me
If this might be a brother.
   Miranda.   I should sin
To think but nobly of my grandmother:
Good wombs have borne bad sons.
   Prospero.   Now the condition. 120
This King of Naples, being an enemy
To me inveterate, hearkens my brother's suit;
Which was, that he, in lieu o' the premises
Of homage and I know not how much tribute,
Should presently extirpate me and mine   125
Out of the dukedom, and confer fair Milan,
With all the honours on my brother: whereon,
A treacherous army levied, one midnight
Fated to the purpose did Antonio open
The gates of Milan; and, i' the dead of darkness,   130
The ministers for the purpose hurried thence
Me and thy crying self.
   Miranda.   Alack, for pity!
I, not rememb'ring how I cried out then,
Will cry it o'er again: it is a hint,

---

112 **dry . . . for sway:** thirsting for sovereign power.   **117**
his condition and the event: the terms he made and what happened.   118 **If this . . . brother:** i.e. if this is the sort of conduct
you would expect of a brother.   119 **but:** except, other than.
123 **in lieu o' the premises:** in consideration of the stipulations.
125 **presently:** immediately.   128 **levied:** (having been) levied.
131 **ministers:** servants, men acting under authority.   **134**
hint: occasion.

That wrings mine eyes to 't.

Prospero.   Hear a little further,   135
And then I'll bring thee to the present business
Which now's upon us; without the which this story
Were most impertinent.

Miranda.   Wherefore did they not
That hour destroy us?

Prospero.   Well demanded, wench:
My tale provokes that question. Dear, they durst not,
So dear the love my people bore me, nor set   141
A mark so bloody on the business; but
With colours fairer painted their foul ends.
In few, they hurried us aboard a bark,
Bore us some leagues to sea; where they prepar'd   145
A rotten carcass of a butt, not rigg'd,
Nor tackle, sail, nor mast; the very rats
Instinctively have quit it: there they hoist us,
To cry to the sea that roar'd to us; to sigh
To the winds whose pity, sighing back again,   150
Did us but loving wrong.

Miranda.   Alack! what trouble
Was I then to you!

Prospero.   O, a cherubin
Thou wast, that did preserve me! Thou didst smile,
Infused with a fortitude from heaven,
When I have deck'd the sea with drops full salt,   155
Under my burden groan'd; which rais'd in me
An undergoing stomach, to bear up

---

135 **wrings:** squeezes the water out of.   **to 't:** i.e. to crying.
138 **impertinent:** irrelevant.   141-2 **nor set . . . business:**
nor (did they dare to) stain themselves with a deed of blood.   144
In few: in short.   146 **butt:** tub. [*N*].   147 **Nor tackle:** i.e.
not having tackle.   148 **have:** vivid for 'had' (historic present).
152 **cherubin:** cherub, angel. [*N*].   155 **deck'd:** adorned. [*N*].
156 **Under:** i.e. (and) under.   **which:** i.e. your smile.   157
undergoing stomach: a resolution to endure.

Against what should ensue.

  Miranda.   How came we ashore?

  Prospero. By Providence divine.

Some food we had and some fresh water that   160

A noble Neapolitan, Gonzalo,

Out of his charity,—who being then appointed

Master of this design,—did give us; with

Rich garments, linens, stuffs, and necessaries,

Which since have steaded much; so, of his gentleness, 165

Knowing I lov'd my books, he furnish'd me,

From mine own library with volumes that

I prize above my dukedom.

  Miranda.   Would I might

But ever see that man!

  Prospero.   Now I arise:—

                           [Resumes his mantle.

Sit still, and hear the last of our sea-sorrow.   170

Here in this island we arriv'd; and here

Have I, thy schoolmaster, made thee more profit

Than other princes can, that have more time

For vainer hours and tutors not so careful.

  Miranda. Heavens thank you for't! And now, I pray

      you, sir—   175

For still 'tis beating in my mind,—your reason

For raising this sea-storm?

  Prospero.   Know thus far forth.

By accident most strange, bountiful Fortune,

Now my dear lady, hath mine enemies

Brought to this shore; and by my prescience   180

I find my zenith doth depend upon

---

   165 steaded: been of use.   **of his gentleness:** in the kindness of his heart.   **172 made thee more profit:** made you
benefit more.   **179 Now my dear lady:** (who is) now my
auspicious mistress (in contrast with what she was formerly).
181 zenith: the highest point (of my fortune). [*N*].

V,
Import
LEARN

A most auspicious star, whose influence
If now I court not but omit, my fortunes
Will ever after droop. Here cease more questions;
Thou art inclin'd to sleep; 'tis a good dulness,   185
And give it way;—I know thou canst not choose.—

         [MIRANDA *sleeps.*

Come away, servant, come! I'm ready now.
Approach, my Ariel; come!

      Enter ARIEL.

 Ariel. All hail, great master! grave sir, hail! I come
To answer thy best pleasure; be't to fly,   190
To swim, to dive into the fire, to ride
On the curl'd clouds: to thy strong bidding task
Ariel and all his quality.
 Prospero.   Hast thou, spirit,
Perform'd to point the tempest that I bade thee?
 Ariel. To every article.   195
I boarded the king's ship; now on the beak,
Now in the waist, the deck, in every cabin,
I flam'd amazement: sometime I'd divide
And burn in many places; on the topmast,
The yards, and boresprit, would I flame distinctly,   200
Then meet, and join: Jove's lightnings, the precursors
O' the dreadful thunder-claps, more momentary
And sight-outrunning were not: the fire and cracks
Of sulphurous roaring the most mighty Neptune
Seem to besiege and make his bold waves tremble,   205
Yea, his dread trident shake.

  186 **give it way:** let it have its course. [*N*]. 192 **to thy strong
bidding:** (in obedience) to thy powerful commands. **task:** set to
work. 193 **quality:** profession (i.e. Ariel's companion spirits).
194 **to point:** precisely. 195 **To every article:** in every detail.
196 **beak:** prow. 197 **waist:** the middle part of the upper deck.
198 **sometime:** sometimes. [*N*]. 200 **boresprit:** bowsprit.
distinctly: separately. 204 **Neptune:** god of the sea.

Prospero.   My brave spirit!
Who was so firm, so constant, that this coil
Would not infect his reason?
  Ariel.   Not a soul
But felt a fever of the mad and play'd
Some tricks of desperation. All but mariners,   210
Plunged in the foaming brine and quit the vessel,
Then all a-fire with me: the king's son, Ferdinand,
With hair up-staring,—then like reeds, not hair,—
Was the first man that leap'd; cried, 'Hell is empty,
And all the devils are here.'
  Prospero.   Why, that's my spirit!   215
But was not this nigh shore?
  Ariel.   Close by, my master.
  Prospero. But are they, Ariel, safe?
  Ariel.   Not a hair perish'd;
On their sustaining garments not a blemish,
But fresher than before: and, as thou bad'st me,
In troops I have dispers'd them 'bout the isle.   220
The king's son have I landed by himself;
Whom I left cooling of the air with sighs
In an odd angle of the isle, and sitting,
His arms in this sad knot.
  Prospero.   Of the king's ship
The mariners, say how thou hast dispos'd,   225
And all the rest o' the fleet.
  Ariel.   Safely in harbour
Is the king's ship; in the deep nook, where once
Thou call'dst me up at midnight to fetch dew
From the still-vex'd Bermoothes; there she's hid:

---

  206 **brave**: fine.   207 **coil**: tumult, confusion.   208
infect: affect injuriously.   209 **of the mad**: such as mad men
feel.   213 **up-staring**: standing on end.   218 **sustaining**:
supporting. [*N*].   223 **angle**: corner.   227 **nook**: creek.
229 **still-vex'd Bermoothes**: constantly disturbed Bermudas. [*N*].

The mariners all under hatches stow'd;   230
Who, with a charm join'd to their suffer'd labour,
I have left asleep: and for the rest o' the fleet
Which I dispers'd, they all have met again,
And are upon the Mediterranean flote,
Bound sadly home for Naples,   235
Supposing that they saw the king's ship wrack'd,
And his great person perish.

Prospero.   Ariel, thy charge
Exactly is perform'd: but there 's more work:
What is the time o' th' day?

Ariel.   Past the mid season.

Prospero. At least two glasses. The time 'twixt six and
    now   240
Must by us both be spent most preciously.

Ariel. Is there more toil? Since thou dost give me pains,
Let me remember thee what thou hast promis'd
Which is not yet perform'd me.

Prospero.   How now! moody?
What is 't thou canst demand?

Ariel.   My liberty.   245

Prospero. Before the time be out? no more!

Ariel.   I prithee
Remember, I have done thee worthy service;
Told thee no lies, made no mistakings, serv'd
Without or grudge or grumblings: thou didst promise
To bate me a full year.

Prospero.   Dost thou forget   250
From what a torment I did free thee?

Ariel.   No.

Prospero. Thou dost; and think'st it much to tread the ooze

---

234 **flote**: sea. [*N*].   239 **the mid season**: noon.   240
glasses: hours. [*N*].   242 **pains**: trouble, tasks.   243
remember: remind.   244 **me**: for me.   249 **grudge**:
complaint.   250 **bate**: remit. [*N*].   252 **much**: a hard task.

Of the salt deep,
To run upon the sharp wind of the north,
To do me business in the veins o' th' earth   255
When it is bak'd with frost.
    Ariel.   I do not, sir.
    Prospero. Thou liest, malignant thing! Hast thou forgot
The foul witch Sycorax, who with age and envy
Was grown into a hoop? hast thou forgot her?
    Ariel. No, sir.
    Prospero.   Thou hast. Where was she born? speak;
        tell me.   260
    Ariel. Sir, in Argier.
    Prospero.   O! was she so? I must,
Once in a month, recount what thou hast been,
Which thou forget'st. This damn'd witch, Sycorax,
For mischiefs manifold and sorceries terrible
To enter human hearing, from Argier,   265
Thou know'st, was banish'd: for one thing she did
They would not take her life. Is not this true?
    Ariel. Ay, sir.
    Prospero. This blue-ey'd hag was hither brought with child,
And here was left by the sailors. Thou, my slave,   270
As thou report'st thyself, wast then her servant:
And, for thou wast a spirit too delicate
To act her earthy and abhorr'd commands,
Refusing her grand hests, she did confine thee,
By help of her more potent ministers,   275
And in her most unmitigable rage,
Into a cloven pine; within which rift
Imprison'd, thou didst painfully remain
A dozen years; within which space she died
And left thee there, where thou didst vent thy groans 280

    258 **envy:** malice.   261 **Argier:** Algiers. [*N*].   272 **for:**
because.   274 **grand hests:** great commands.   275
ministers: cf. l. 131, above.

As fast as mill-wheels strike. Then was this island,—
Save for the son that she did litter here,
A freckled whelp hag-born,—not honour'd with
A human shape.

   Ariel.   Yes; Caliban her son.

  Prospero. Dull thing, I say so; he that Caliban,   285
Whom now I keep in service. Thou best know'st
What torment I did find thee in; thy groans
Did make wolves howl and penetrate the breasts
Of ever-angry bears: it was a torment
To lay upon the damn'd, which Sycorax   290
Could not again undo; it was mine art,
When I arriv'd and heard thee, that made gape
The pine, and let thee out.

   Ariel.   I thank thee, master.

  Prospero. If thou more murmur'st, I will rend an oak
And peg thee in his knotty entrails till   295
Thou hast howl'd away twelve winters.

   Ariel.   Pardon, master;
I will be correspondent to command,
And do my spiriting gently.

  Prospero.   Do so; and after two days
I will discharge thee.

   Ariel.   That's my noble master!
What shall I do? say what? what shall I do?   300

  Prospero. Go make thyself like a nymph of the sea: be
    subject
To no sight but thine and mine; invisible
To every eyeball else. Go, take this shape,
And hither come in 't: go, hence with diligence!

                          [*Exit* ARIEL.
Awake, dear heart, awake! thou hast slept well;   305
Awake!

---

297 **correspondent**: submissive.   298 **spiriting**: work of a
spirit. **gently**: courteously. [*N*].

Miranda. [*Waking.*] The strangeness of your story put
Heaviness in me.

Prospero.   Shake it off. Come on;
We'll visit Caliban my slave, who never
Yields us kind answer.

Miranda.   'Tis a villain, sir,
I do not love to look on.

Prospero.   But, as 'tis,   310
We cannot miss him: he does make our fire,
Fetch in our wood; and serves in offices
That profit us.—What ho! slave! Caliban!
Thou earth, thou! speak.

Caliban. [*Within.*]   There's wood enough within.

Prospero. Come forth, I say; there's other business for
thee:
                                                       315
Come, thou tortoise! when?

Re-enter ARIEL, *like a water-nymph.*

Fine apparition! My quaint Ariel,
Hark in thine ear.

Ariel.   My lord, it shall be done.   [*Exit.*

Prospero. Thou poisonous slave, got by the devil himself
Upon thy wicked dam, come forth!   320

Enter CALIBAN.

Caliban. As wicked dew as e'er my mother brush'd
With raven's feather from unwholesome fen
Drop on you both! a south-west blow on ye,
And blister you all o'er!

  306 Heaviness: drowsiness.   311 miss: do without.
314 Thou earth: i.e. you lump of earth. [*N*].   316 when?:
an exclamation of impatience—'How long am I to wait for you?'
317 quaint: dainty,   319 got: begotten.

Prospero. For this, be sure, to-night thou shalt have
cramps,   325
Side-stitches that shall pen thy breath up; urchins
Shall for that vast of night that they may work
All exercise on thee: thou shalt be pinch'd
As thick as honeycomb, each pinch more stinging
Than bees that made 'em.
  Caliban.   I must eat my dinner   330
This island's mine, by Sycorax my mother,
Which thou tak'st from me. When thou camest first,
Thou strok'dst me, and made much of me; wouldst
give me
Water with berries in't; and teach me how
To name the bigger light, and how the less,   335
That burn by day and night: and then I lov'd thee
And show'd thee all the qualities o' th' isle,
The fresh springs, brine-pits, barren place, and fertile.
Cursed be I that did so!—All the charms
Of Sycorax, toads, beetles, bats, light on you!   340
For I am all the subjects that you have,
Which first was mine own king; and here you sty me
In this hard rock, whiles you do keep from me
The rest o' th' island.
  Prospero.   Thou most lying slave,
Whom stripes may move, not kindness! I have us'd
thee,   345
Filth as thou art, with human care; and lodg'd thee
In mine own cell, till thou didst seek to violate
The honour of my child.

---

325 **cramps**: rheumatic pains.   326 **urchins**: hedgehogs. [*N*].
327 **for that vast of night**: during that empty part in the middle of
the night when men are asleep.   **that they**: when they. [*N*].   328
exercise on: practise on, torment.   330 **'em**: the cells of the
honeycomb. [*N*].   331 **by**: by right of inheritance from.
342 **sty**: confine like a pig in a sty, pen up.

Caliban. Oh ho! Oh ho!—would it had been done!
Thou didst prevent me; I had peopled else   350
This isle with Calibans.

  Prospero.   Abhorred slave,
Which any print of goodness will not take,
Being capable of all ill! I pitied thee,
Took pains to make thee speak, taught thee each hour
One thing or other: when thou didst not, savage,   355
Know thine own meaning, but wouldst gabble like
A thing most brutish, I endow'd thy purposes
With words that made them known: but thy vile race,
Though thou didst learn, had that in't which good
    natures
Could not abide to be with; therefore wast thou   360
Deservedly confin'd into this rock,
Who hadst deserv'd more than a prison.

  Caliban. You taught me language; and my profit on't
Is, I know how to curse: the red plague rid you,
For learning me your language!

  Prospero.   Hag-seed, hence!   365
Fetch us in fuel; and be quick, thou'rt best,
To answer other business. Shrug'st thou, malice?
If thou neglect'st, or dost unwillingly
What I command, I'll rack thee with old cramps,
Fill all thy bones with aches; make thee roar,   370
That beasts shall tremble at thy din.

  Caliban.   No, pray thee!—
[*Aside.*] I must obey: his art is of such power,
It would control my dam's god, Setebos,
And make a vassal of him.

---

363 **on't**: of, from it.   364 **rid**: destroy. [*N*].   365 **learning**:
teaching (as still in colloquial usage).   **Hag-seed**:
witch's offspring.   366 **thou'rt best**: thou wert best, i.e. 'or
it will be the worse for you'.   369 **old**: of old age (cf. IV. i.
258). [*N*].

ACT I SCENE II

Prospero.   So, slave; hence!

[*Exit* CALIBAN.

Re-enter ARIEL *invisible, playing and singing;* FERDIN-
AND *following.*

ARIEL'S SONG.

Come unto these yellow sands,   375
    And then take hands:
Curtsied when you have, and kiss'd,—
    The wild waves whist,—
Foot it featly here and there;
And, sweet sprites, the burden bear.   380
    Hark, hark!
                [*Burden:* Bow, wow, *dispersedly.*
    The watch-dogs bark:
                [*Burden:* Bow,wow, *dispersedly.*
    Hark, hark! I hear
The strain of strutting Chanticleer
            Cry, Cock-a-diddle-dow.

Ferdinand. Where should this music be? i' th' air, or th'
    earth?   385
It sounds no more;—and sure, it waits upon
Some god o' th' island. Sitting on a bank,
Weeping again the king my father's wrack,
This music crept by me upon the waters,
Allaying both their fury, and my passion,   390
With its sweet air: thence I have follow'd it,—
Or it hath drawn me rather,—but 'tis gone.
No, it begins again.

378 whist: being hushed, silent. [*N*].   379 Foot it featly:
dance nimbly.   380 the burden bear: join in the chorus.
386 waits upon: attends (i.e. is being played for).   388 again:
over and over again.   390 passion: grief.

ARIEL *sings.*

Full fathom five thy father lies;
    Of his bones are coral made: 395
Those are pearls that were his eyes:
    Nothing of him that doth fade,
But doth suffer a sea-change
Into something rich and strange.
Sea-nymphs hourly ring his knell: 400
            [*Burden:* ding-dong.
    Hark! now I hear them,—ding-dong, bell.

Ferdinand. The ditty does remember my drown'd father.
This is no mortal business, nor no sound
That the earth owes:—I hear it now above me.
    Prospero. The fringed curtains of thine eye advance,   405
And say what thou seest yond.
    Miranda.   What is 't? a spirit?
Lord, how it looks about! Believe me, sir,
It carries a brave form:—but 'tis a spirit.
    Prospero. No, wench; it eats and sleeps, and hath such
        senses
As we have, such; this gallant which thou see'st,   410
Was in the wrack; and, but he's something stain'd
With grief,—that's beauty's canker—thou might'st call him
A goodly person: he hath lost his fellows
And strays about to find 'em.
    Miranda.   I might call him
A thing divine; for nothing natural   415
I ever saw so noble.
    Prospero. [*Aside.*] It goes on, I see,

402 **remember:** commemorate.   403 **no mortal business:**
not the work of mortals.   404 **owes:** owns, possesses.   406
yond: yonder.   408 **brave:** noble (cf. I. ii. 6, &c.). [*N*].   **form:**
outward appearance.   411 **but:** except (for the fact that).
something: somewhat.   412 **that's beauty's canker:** that
destroys beauty. [*N*].   415 **natural:** in nature (not in the
world of spirits).   416 **It:** i.e. my plan.

As my soul prompts it.—Spirit, fine spirit! I'll free thee
Within two days for this.

Ferdinand.   Most sure, the goddess
On whom these airs attend!—Vouchsafe, my prayer
May know if you remain upon this island;   420
And that you will some good instruction give
How I may bear me here: my prime request,
Which I do last pronounce, is,—O you wonder!—
If you be maid or no?

Miranda.   No wonder, sir;
But certainly a maid.

Ferdinand.   My language! heavens!—   425
I am the best of them that speak this speech,
Were I but where 'tis spoken.

Prospero.   How! the best?
What wert thou, if the King of Naples heard thee?

Ferdinand. A single thing, as I am now, that wonders
To hear thee speak of Naples. He does hear me;   430
And, that he does, I weep: myself am Naples,
Who with mine eyes,—ne'er since at ebb,—beheld
The king my father wrack'd.

Miranda.   Alack, for mercy!

Ferdinand. Yes, faith, and all his lords; the Duke of Milan,
And his brave son being twain.

Prospero.   [*Aside.*] The Duke of Milan,   435
And his more braver daughter could control thee,
If now 'twere fit to do 't.—At the first sight   [*Aside.*]
They have changed eyes:—delicate Ariel,

420 **remain:** dwell.   422 **bear me:** conduct myself.
prime: chief.   429 **single:** solitary. [*N*].   430 **Naples:**
i.e. the King of Naples.   **He does hear me:** He (the King of
Naples) hears me (i.e. I, Ferdinand, who am now King, hear the King
speak when I hear myself speak).   432 **at ebb:** free from tears.
435 **twain:** two (of them). [*N*].   436 **control:** challenge, confute.
438 **changed eyes:** fallen in love (because lovers see with one
another's eyes; *not* 'exchanged glances').

I'll set thee free for this!—[*To* FERDINAND.] A word,
    good sir;
I fear you have done yourself some wrong: a word.   440
  Mira. [*Aside.*] Why speaks my father so ungently? This
Is the third man that e'er I saw; the first
That e'er I sigh'd for: pity move my father
To be inclin'd my way!
  Ferdinand.   [*Aside.*] O! if a virgin,
And your affection not gone forth, I'll make you   445
The Queen of Naples.
  Prospero.   Soft, sir: one word more—
[*Aside.*] They are both in either's powers: but this swift
    business
I must uneasy make, lest too light winning
Make the prize light.—[*To* FERDINAND.] One word more:
    I charge thee
That thou attend me. Thou dost here usurp   450
The name thou ow'st not; and hast put thyself
Upon this island as a spy, to win it
From me, the lord on 't.
  Ferdinand.   No, as I am a man.
  Miranda. There's nothing ill can dwell in such a temple:
If the ill spirit have so fair a house,   455
Good things will strive to dwell with 't.
  Prospero.   [*To* FERDINAND.] Follow me.—
[*To* MIRANDA.] Speak not you for him; he's a traitor.—
    [*To* FERDINAND.] Come;
I'll manacle thy neck and feet together:
Sea-water shalt thou drink; thy food shall be
The fresh-brook mussels, wither'd roots and husks   460
Wherein the acorn cradled. Follow.

---

    440 **you have ... wrong**: you are mistaken.   445 **gone forth**:
engaged.   447 **either's**: one another's.   448 **light**: easy.
449 **light**: of little value.   450 **attend**: pay attention to, listen to.
451 **ow'st**: own, possess.   453 **on 't**: of it (cf. I. ii. 87, &c.).

Ferdinand.   No;
I will resist such entertainment till
Mine enemy has more power.
                [*He draws, and is charmed from moving.*
  Miranda.   O dear father!
Make not too rash a trial of him, for
He's gentle, and not fearful.
  Prospero.   What! I say,   465
My foot my tutor?—Put thy sword up, traitor;
Who mak'st a show, but dar'st not strike, thy conscience
Is so possess'd with guilt: come from thy ward,
For I can here disarm thee with this stick
And make thy weapon drop.
  Miranda.   Beseech you, father!   470
  Prospero. Hence! hang not on my garments.
  Miranda.   Sir, have pity:
I'll be his surety.
  Prospero.   Silence! one word more
Shall make me chide thee, if not hate thee. What!
An advocate for an impostor? hush!
Thou think'st there is no more such shapes as he,   475
Having seen but him and Caliban: foolish wench!
To the most of men this is a Caliban
And they to him are angels.
  Miranda.   My affections
Are then most humble; I have no ambition
To see a goodlier man.
  Prospero. [*To* FERDINAND.] Come on; obey: 480
Thy nerves are in their infancy again,
And have no vigour in them.

---

465 **He's gentle . . . fearful**: *either* (a) He is of gentle birth, and
not a coward, *or* (b) He is not violent, and not terrifying.   466
My foot my tutor?: Am I to take lessons from my inferior? (The
foot is lower than, 'inferior to', the head.)   468 **ward**: posture
of defence (in fencing).   481 **nerves**: sinews.

Ferdinand.   So they are:
My spirits, as in a dream, are all bound up.
My father's loss, the weakness which I feel,
The wrack of all my friends, nor this man's threats,   485
To whom I am subdued, are but light to me,
Might I but through my prison once a day
Behold this maid: all corners else o' th' earth
Let liberty make use of; space enough
Have I in such a prison.
   Prospero.   [*Aside.*] It works.—[*To* FERDINAND.] Come
    on.—   490
Thou hast done well, fine Ariel!—[*To* FERDINAND.] Follow
    me.—
[*To* ARIEL.] Hark, what thou else shalt do me.
   Miranda.   Be of comfort;
My father's of a better nature, sir,
Than he appears by speech: this is unwonted,
Which now came from him.
   Prospero.   Thou shalt be as free   495
As mountain winds; but then exactly do
All points of my command.
   Ariel.   To the syllable.
   Prospero. [*To* FERDINAND.] Come, follow.—Speak not
    for him.   [*Exeunt.*

---

488 else: other.   **489 liberty:** i.e. men who are free.   **492**
what thou else &c: what other (service) thou &c.   **497 To**
the syllable: in exact detail.

ACT II

Scene I. ANOTHER PART OF THE ISLAND.

Enter ALONSO, SEBASTIAN, ANTONIO, GONZALO, ADRIAN, FRANCISCO, *and others.*

Gonzalo. Beseech you, sir, be merry: you have cause,
So have we all, of joy; for our escape
Is much beyond our loss. Our hint of woe
Is common: every day some sailor's wife,
The masters of some merchant and the merchant,   5
Have just our theme of woe; but for the miracle,
I mean our preservation, few in millions
Can speak like us: then wisely, good sir, weigh
Our sorrow with our comfort.
 Alonso.   Prithee, peace.
 Sebastian. He receives comfort like cold porridge.   10
 Antonio. The visitor will not give him o'er so.
 Sebastian. Look, he's winding up the watch of his wit; by and by it will strike.
 Gonzalo. Sir,—
 Sebastian. One: tell.   15
 Gonzalo. When every grief is entertain'd that's offer'd,
Comes to the entertainer—
 Sebastian. A dollar.
 Gonzalo. Dolour comes to him, indeed: you have spoken truer than you purposed.   20
 Sebastian. You have taken it wiselier than I meant you should.
 Gonzalo. Therefore, my lord,—

3 **hint**: occasion (cf. I. ii. 134).   5 **some merchant**: some merchant vessel.   6 **theme of woe**: subject for grief.   15 **tell**: count. [*N*].   16 **When . . . offer'd**: when a man takes every opportunity of grieving that presents itself.

Antonio. Fie, what a spendthrift is he of his tongue!

Alonso. I prithee, spare.   25

Gonzalo. Well, I have done: but yet—

Sebastian. He will be talking.

Antonio. Which, of he or Adrian, for a good wager, first begins to crow?

Sebastian. The old cock.   30

Antonio. The cockerel.

Sebastian. Done. The wager?

Antonio. A laughter.

Sebastian. A match!

Adrian. Though this island seem to be desert,—   35

Sebastian. Ha, ha, ha! So you're paid.

Adrian. Uninhabitable, and almost inaccessible,—

Sebastian. Yet—

Adrian. Yet—

Antonio. He could not miss it.   40

Adrian. It must needs be of subtle, tender, and delicate temperance.

Antonio. Temperance was a delicate wench.

Sebastian. Ay, and a subtle; as he most learnedly delivered.   45

Adrian. The air breathes upon us here most sweetly.

Sebastian. As if it had lungs, and rotten ones.

Antonio. Or as 'twere perfumed by a fen.

Gonzalo. Here is everything advantageous to life.

Antonio. True; save means to live.   50

Sebastian. Of that there's none, or little.

Gonzalo. How lush and lusty the grass looks! how green!

---

25 **spare**: i.e. spare your words, desist.   30 **The old cock**: i.e. Gonzalo.   31 **The cockerel**: i.e. Adrian.   33 **laughter**: (1) a laugh, (2) the whole number of eggs laid by a hen before she is ready to 'sit'.   34 **A match!**: It's a bet!   36 **you're paid**: you've won.   42 **temperance**: temperature.

Antonio. The ground indeed is tawny.

Sebastian. With an eye of green in 't.   55

Antonio. He misses not much.

Sebastian. No; he doth but mistake the truth totally.

Gonzalo. But the rarity of it is,—which is indeed almost beyond credit,—

Sebastian. As many vouch'd rarities are.   60

Gonzalo. That our garments, being, as they were, drenched in the sea, hold notwithstanding their freshness and glosses; being rather new-dyed than stain'd with salt water.

Antonio. If but one of his pockets could speak, would it not say he lies?   65

Sebastian. Ay, or very falsely pocket up his report.

Gonzalo. Methinks, our garments are now as fresh as when we put them on first in Afric, at the marriage of the king's fair daughter Claribel to the King of Tunis.

Sebastian. 'Twas a sweet marriage, and we prosper well in our return.   71

Adrian. Tunis was never graced before with such a paragon to their queen.

Gonzalo. Not since widow Dido's time.

Antonio. Widow! a pox o' that! How came that widow in? Widow Dido!   76

Sebastian. What if he had said, widower Æneas too? Good Lord, how you take it!

Adrian. Widow Dido, said you? you make me study of that: she was of Carthage, not of Tunis.   80

Gonzalo. This Tunis, sir, was Carthage.

Adrian. Carthage?

Gonzalo. I assure you, Carthage.

Antonio. His word is more than the miraculous harp.

54 **indeed**: in actual fact (Antonio is contradicting, not agreeing with Gonzalo).   55 **eye**: spot.   56 **He misses not much**: he is not far wrong (ironical).   66 **pocket up**: conceal.   73 **to**: for, as.   79 **study of**: think intently about, reflect about.

Sebastian. He hath rais'd the wall, and houses too.   85

Antonio. What impossible matter will he make easy next?

Sebastian. I think he will carry this island home in his pocket, and give it his son for an apple.

Antonio. And, sowing the kernels of it in the sea, bring forth more islands.   90

Alonso. Ay?

Antonio. Why, in good time.

Gonzalo. [*To* ALONSO.] Sir, we were talking that our garments seem now as fresh as when we were at Tunis at the marriage of your daughter, who is now queen.   95

Antonio. And the rarest that e'er came there.

Sebastian. Bate, I beseech you, widow Dido.

Antonio. O! widow Dido; ay, widow Dido.

Gonzalo. Is not, sir, my doublet as fresh as the first day I wore it? I mean, in a sort.   100

Antonio. That sort was well fish'd for.

Gonzalo. When I wore it at your daughter's marriage?

Alonso. You cram these words into mine ears, against
The stomach of my sense. Would I had never
Married my daughter there! for, coming thence,   105
My son is lost; and, in my rate, she too,
Who is so far from Italy remov'd,
I ne'er again shall see her. O thou, mine heir
Of Naples and of Milan! what strange fish
Hath made his meal on thee?

Francisco.   Sir, he may live: 110
I saw him beat the surges under him,
And ride upon their backs: he trod the water,
Whose enmity he flung aside, and breasted
The surge most swoln that met him: his bold head
'Bove the contentious waves he kept, and oar'd   115

---

91 **Ay?**: what is that you say? [*N*].   97 **Bate**: except.
104 **The stomach of my sense**: the inclination of my sense (of hearing).   106 **rate**: opinion.

Himself with his good arms in lusty stroke
To the shore, that o'er his wave-worn basis bow'd,
As stooping to relieve him. I not doubt
He came alive to land.

   Alonso.   No, no; he's gone.

   Sebastian. Sir, you may thank yourself for this great loss,
That would not bless our Europe with your daughter,   121
But rather loose her to an African;
Where she at least is banish'd from your eye,
Who hath cause to wet the grief on 't.

   Alonso.   Prithee, peace.

   Sebastian. You were kneel'd to and importun'd otherwise
By all of us; and the fair soul herself   126
Weigh'd between loathness and obedience, at
Which end o' the beam should bow. We have lost your son,
I fear, for ever: Milan and Naples have
Mo widows in them of this business' making,   130
Than we bring men to comfort them: the fault's
Your own.

   Alonso. So is the dearest of the loss.

   Gonzalo. My lord Sebastian,
The truth you speak doth lack some gentleness
And time to speak it in; you rub the sore,   135
When you should bring the plaster.

   Sebastian.   Very well.

   Antonio. And most chirurgeonly.

---

117 **his:** its (referring to the shore) [*N*].   **basis:** base, edge.
122 **loose her:** mate her with. [*N*].   123 **she . . . banish'd:**
at any rate she is banished (if not lost altogether).   124 **Who
hath . . . on 't:** who has reason to weep for it. [*N*].   127 **Weigh'd
between loathness:** balanced between unwillingness. [*N*].   130
Mo: more.   **widows:** i.e. widows who will not receive their husbands again on account of this voyage and its results. [*N*].   132
dearest: hardest, severest. [*N*].   135 **time:** i.e. a fitting time.
136 **Very well:** i.e. very well said. (Sebastian speaks ironically.)
137 **chirurgeonly:** like a surgeon.

Gonzalo. It is foul weather in us all, good sir,
When you are cloudy.
   Sebastian.   Foul weather?
   Antonio.   Very foul.
   Gonzalo. Had I plantation of this isle, my lord,—   140
   Antonio. He'd sow 't with nettle-seed.
   Sebastian.   Or docks, or mallows.
   Gonzalo. And were the king on 't, what would I do?
   Sebastian. 'Scape being drunk for want of wine.
   Gonzalo. I' the commonwealth I would by contraries
Execute all things; for no kind of traffic   145
Would I admit; no name of magistrate;
Letters should not be known; riches, poverty,
And use of service, none; contract, succession,
Bourn, bound of land, tilth, vineyard, none;
No use of metal, corn, or wine, or oil;   150
No occupation; all men idle, all;
And women too, but innocent and pure;
No sovereignty,—
   Sebastian.   Yet he would be king on 't.
   Antonio. The latter end of his commonwealth forgets the
beginning.   155
   Gonzalo. All things in common nature should produce
Without sweat or endeavour: treason, felony,
Sword, pike, knife, gun, or need of any engine,
Would I not have; but nature should bring forth,
Of it own kind, all foison, all abundance,   160
To feed my innocent people.
   Sebastian. No marrying 'mong his subjects?

---

   139 cloudy: gloomy. [*N*].   **140 plantation:** colonization. [*N*].
144 by contraries: in the opposite manner to what is usual.   **145
traffic:** trade. [*N*].   **147 Letters:** learning.   **149 Bourn:** boun-
dary.   **bound of land:** landmark.   **tilth:** land under cultivation.
152 but innocent &c.: i.e. although idle. See l. 163 and [*N*].
158 engine: engine of war (or, possibly, of torture).   **160 it
own:** its own.   **foison:** plenty.

Antonio. None, man; all idle; whores and knaves.

Gonzalo. I would with such perfection govern, sir,
To excel the golden age.

Sebastian.   'Save his majesty!   165

Antonio. Long live Gonzalo!

Gonzalo.   And,—do you mark me, sir?

Alonso. Prithee, no more: thou dost talk nothing to me.

Gonzalo. I do well believe your highness; and did it to
minister occasion to these gentlemen, who are of such
sensible and nimble lungs that they always use to laugh at
nothing.   171

Antonio. 'Twas you we laugh'd at.

Gonzalo. Who in this kind of merry fooling am nothing to
you; so you may continue and laugh at nothing still.

Antonio. What a blow was there given!   175

Sebastian. And it had not fallen flat-long.

Gonzalo. You are gentlemen of brave mettle: you would
lift the moon out of her sphere, if she would continue in it
five weeks without changing.

Enter ARIEL, *invisible, playing solemn music.*

Sebastian. We would so, and then go a-bat-fowling.   180

Antonio. Nay, good my lord, be not angry.

Gonzalo. No, I warrant you; I will not adventure my
discretion so weakly. Will you laugh me asleep, for I am
very heavy?

163 **idle**: vain, worthless [*N*].   165 **To**: as to.   **'Save**:
God save. [*N*].   167 **nothing**: nonsense, trifles.   170 **sensible**: sensitive.   **use to**: are accustomed to.   176 **And**:
if.   **flat-long**: with the flat of the sword (i.e. harmlessly).
177–9. **You are . . . changing**: i.e. you are such lively gentlemen
that you can endure nothing serious or regular. [*N*].   180 **a-bat-
fowling**: catching birds at night. [*N*].   182–3 **adventure my
discretion**: risk losing my reputation for good sense.   184
heavy: sleepy,

Antonio. Go sleep, and hear us.   185

       [*All sleep but* ALONSO, SEBASTIÁN, *and* ANTONIO.

Alonso. What! all so soon asleep! I wish mine eyes

Would, with themselves, shut up my thoughts: I find

They are inclin'd to do so.

  Sebastian.   Please you, sir,

Do not omit the heavy offer of it:

It seldom visits sorrow; when it doth   190

It is a comforter.

  Antonio.   We two, my lord,

Will guard your person while you take your rest,

And watch your safety.

  Alonso.   Thank you. Wondrous heavy.

          [ALONSO *sleeps. Exit* ARIEL.

Sebastian. What a strange drowsiness possesses them!

Antonio. It is the quality o' the climate.

  Sebastian.   Why   195

Doth it not then our eyelids sink? I find not

Myself dispos'd to sleep.

  Antonio.   Nor I: my spirits are nimble.

They fell together all, as by consent;

They dropp'd, as by a thunder-stroke. What might,

Worthy Sebastian? O! what might?—No more:—   200

And yet methinks I see it in thy face,

What thou should'st be. The occasion speaks thee; and

My strong imagination sees a crown

Dropping upon thy head.

  Sebastian.   What! art thou waking?

Antonio. Do you not hear me speak?

  Sebastian.   I do; and surely, 205

It is a sleepy language, and thou speak'st

---

  188 do so: viz. shut themselves.   **189 it:** i.e. sleep.   196
sink: (trans.) cause to sink.   **198 They fell ... consent:**
i.e. Alonso, Gonzalo, &c., fell asleep as if by agreement.   202
speaks: calls.

Out of thy sleep. What is it thou didst say?
This is a strange repose, to be asleep
With eyes wide open; standing, speaking, moving,
And yet so fast asleep.

    Antonio.   Noble Sebastian,   210
Thou let'st thy fortune sleep—die rather; wink'st
Whiles thou art waking.

    Sebastian.   Thou dost snore distinctly:
There's meaning in thy snores.

    Antonio. I am more serious than my custom: you
Must be so too, if heed me; which to do   215
Trebles thee o'er.

    Sebastian.   Well; I am standing water.

    Antonio. I'll teach you how to flow.

    Sebastian.   Do so: to ebb,
Hereditary sloth instructs me.

    Antonio.   O!
If you but knew how you the purpose cherish
Whiles thus you mock it! how, in stripping it,   220
You more invest it! Ebbing men, indeed,
Most often do so near the bottom run
By their own fear or sloth.

    Sebastian.   Prithee, say on:
The setting of thine eye and cheek proclaim
A matter from thee, and a birth indeed   225
Which throes thee much to yield.

    Antonio.   Thus, sir:

---

    211 **wink'st:** sleep'st.   212 **distinctly:** articulately. [*N*].   215
if heed me: if you mean to heed me.   216 **Trebles thee o'er:**
makes you three times as great. [*N*].   **standing:** not flowing.
[*N*].   219–21 **If you . . . invest it!:** If you only knew how by
jesting in this way you make the design (which Antonio has in mind)
seem more desirable; and how by stripping it of its seriousness you
clothe it in greater seriousness. [*N*].   224 **setting:** fixity.   225
A matter: a matter of importance.   226 **throes . . . yield:**
agonizes, causes you much pain to utter. [*N*].

Although this lord of weak remembrance, this
Who shall be of as little memory
When he is earth'd, hath here almost persuaded,—
For he's a spirit of persuasion, only   230
Professes to persuade,—the king, his son's alive,
'Tis as impossible that he's undrown'd
As he that sleeps here swims.
　Sebastian.　　　　　　　I have no hope
That he's undrown'd.
　Antonio.　　　　　O! out of that 'no hope'
What great hope have you! no hope that way is   235
Another way so high a hope that even
Ambition cannot pierce a wink beyond,
But doubts discovery there. Will you grant with me
That Ferdinand is drown'd?
　Sebastian.　　　　　　　He's gone.
　Antonio.　　　　　　　　Then tell me
Who's the next heir of Naples?
　Sebastian.　　　　　　　Claribel.   240
　Antonio. She that is Queen of Tunis; she that dwells
Ten leagues beyond man's life; she that from Naples
Can have no note, unless the sun were post—
The man i' th' moon's too slow—till new-born chins
Be rough and razorable: she that from whom   245

227 **remembrance:** memory, i.e. faculty of remembering. [*N*].
228 **as little memory:** as little remembered (as he remembers
things). 229 **earth'd:** buried. 233 **As he:** i.e. as it is that he.
235–7 **no hope ... beyond:** no hope that Ferdinand is alive means
so high a hope in another direction (i.e. for your prospects), that
ambition cannot see the slightest degree further ahead. 238 **But
doubts ... there:** but is doubtful of being able to discover anything
there (i.e. beyond). [*N*]. **grant:** admit, acknowledge 242 **Ten
leagues ... life:** ten leagues farther (from Naples) than a man
could travel in a life-time. 243 **note:** information. **post:**
messenger. [*N*]. 244–5 **till new-born ... razorable:** till
infants have grown to manhood and are fit to be shaved. 245
she that from whom: she, in coming from whom. [*N*].

We all were sea-swallow'd, though some cast again,
And by that destiny to perform an act
Whereof what's past is prologue, what to come
In yours and my discharge.
   Sebastian.   What stuff is this!—How say you?
'Tis true my brother's daughter's Queen of Tunis;   250
So is she heir of Naples; 'twixt which regions
There is some space.
   Antonio.   A space whose every cubit
Seems to cry out, 'How shall that Claribel
Measure us back to Naples?—Keep in Tunis,
And let Sebastian wake!'—Say, this were death   255
That now hath seiz'd them; why, they were no worse
Than now they are. There be that can rule Naples
As well as he that sleeps; lords that can prate
As amply and unnecessarily
As this Gonzalo; I myself could make   260
A chough of as deep chat. O, that you bore
The mind that I do! what a sleep were this
For your advancement! Do you understand me?
   Sebastian. Methinks I do.
   Antonio.   And how does your content
Tender your own good fortune?
   Sebastian.   I remember   265
You did supplant your brother Prospero.
   Antonio.   True:

246 **though . . . again:** though some (of us were) cast (up) again.
cast: vomited. [*N*].   247 **by that destiny to:** destined by that
fortune to.   248–9 **what to come . . . discharge:** what is to
come depends upon what you and I perform.   249 **discharge:**
performance (a theatrical term).   252 **cubit:** a measure of about
one and a half feet.   254 **us:** i.e. the cubits. **Keep:** remain.
255 **Say, this were death:** i.e. suppose this sleep (of Alonso, &c.)
were death.   260–1 **make . . . chat:** prove myself a crow that
prates as profoundly.   264–5 **And how . . . fortune?:** and how
does your happiness cherish your own good fortune? [*N*].

And look how well my garments sit upon me;
Much feater than before; my brother's servants
Were then my fellows; now they are my men.
  Sebastian. But, for your conscience,—   270
  Antonio. Ay, sir; where lies that? if it were a kibe,
'Twould put me to my slipper; but I feel not
This deity in my bosom: twenty consciences,
That stand 'twixt me and Milan, candied be they,
And melt ere they molest! Here lies your brother,   275
No better than the earth he lies upon,
If he were that which now he's like, that's dead;
Whom I, with this obedient steel,—three inches of it,—
Can lay to bed for ever; whiles you, doing thus,
To the perpetual wink for aye might put   280
This ancient morsel, this Sir Prudence, who
Should not upbraid our course. For all the rest,
They'll take suggestion as a cat laps milk;
They'll tell the clock to any business that
We say befits the hour.
  Sebastian.   Thy case, dear friend,   285
Shall be my precedent: as thou got'st Milan,
I'll come by Naples. Draw thy sword: one stroke
Shall free thee from the tribute which thou pay'st,
And I the king shall love thee.
  Antonio.   Draw together;
And when I rear my hand, do you the like,   290
To fall it on Gonzalo.
  Sebastian.   O! but one word. [*They converse apart.*

268 **feater:** better-fitting.   269 **fellows:** companions.
men: servants.   271-2 **if it were . . . slipper:** if it were
a chilblain on the heel it would force me to wear a slipper.   274
candied: (probably) coated with sugar. [*N*].   280 **perpetual
wink:** everlasting sleep, i.e. death.   281-2 **who . . . upbraid:** so that he should not (then) reprove. [*N*].   284 **They'll
tell the clock:** they'll chime in with, acquiesce in.   291
fall: let fall.

Music. Re-enter ARIEL, *invisible.*

Ariel. My master through his art foresees the danger
That you, his friend, are in; and sends me forth—
For else his project dies—to keep thee living.
> [*Sings in* GONZALO'S *ear.*

> While you here do snoring lie,   295
> Open-ey'd Conspiracy
>   His time doth take.
> If of life you keep a care,
> Shake off slumber, and beware:
>   Awake! awake!   300

Antonio. Then let us both be sudden.
Gonzalo.   Now, good angels
Preserve the king!   [*They wake.*
Alonso. Why, how now! ho, awake! Why are you drawn?
Wherefore this ghastly looking?
Gonzalo.   What's the matter?
Sebastian. Whiles we stood here securing your repose,
Even now, we heard a hollow burst of bellowing   306
Like bulls, or rather lions; did 't not wake you?
It struck mine ear most terribly.
Alonso.   I heard nothing.
Antonio. O! 'twas a din to fright a monster's ear,
To make an earthquake: sure it was the roar   310
Of a whole herd of lions.
Alonso.   Heard you this, Gonzalo?
Gonzalo. Upon mine honour, sir, I heard a humming,
And that a strange one too, which did awake me.
I shak'd you, sir, and cry'd; as mine eyes open'd,   315
I saw their weapons drawn:—there was a noise,
That's verily. 'Tis best we stand upon our guard,

---

297 **time**: opportunity.   298 **keep**: have   301 **sudden**:
swift.   303 **drawn**: with drawn swords.   304 **looking**:
expression.   317 **That's verily**: that's a fact.

Or that we quit this place: let's draw our weapons.

Alonso. Lead off this ground, and let's make further search
For my poor son.   320

Gonzalo. Heavens keep him from these beasts!
For he is, sure, i' the island.

Alonso.   Lead away. [*Exit with the others.*

Ariel. Prospero my lord shall know what I have done:
So, king, go safely on to seek thy son.   [*Exit.*

Scene II. ANOTHER PART OF THE ISLAND

> *Enter* CALIBAN, *with a burden of wood. A noise of
> thunder heard.*

Caliban. All the infections that the sun sucks up
From bogs, fens, flats, on Prosper fall, and make him
By inch-meal a disease! His spirits hear me,
And yet I needs must curse. But they'll nor pinch,
Fright me with urchin-shows, pitch me i' the mire,   5
Nor lead me, like a firebrand, in the dark
Out of my way, unless he bid 'em; but
For every trifle are they set upon me:
Sometime like apes, that mow and chatter at me
And after bite me; then like hedge-hogs, which   10
Lie tumbling in my bare-foot way and mount
Their pricks at my foot-fall; sometime am I
All wound with adders, who with cloven tongues
Do hiss me into madness.—

> *Enter* TRINCULO.

Lo now! lo!
Here comes a spirit of his, and to torment me   15

3 **By inch-meal:** inch by inch.   4 **nor:** neither.   5
urchin-shows: apparitions of hobgoblins.   **pitch:** both (1) toss,
and (2) smear as with pitch.   9 **mow:** make mouths.   11–12
mount Their pricks: erect their prickles.   13 **wound:** twined
about with (from the verb 'wind').

For bringing wood in slowly: I'll fall flat;
Perchance he will not mind me.

Trinculo. Here's neither bush nor shrub to bear off any
weather at all, and another storm brewing; I hear it
sing i' the wind: yond same black cloud, yond huge one, 20
looks like a foul bombard that would shed his liquor. If
it should thunder as it did before, I know not where to
hide my head: yond same cloud cannot choose but fall
by pailfuls.—What have we here? a man or a fish?
Dead or alive? A fish: he smells like a fish; a very 25
ancient and fish-like smell; a kind of not of the newest
Poor-John. A strange fish! Were I in England now,—
as once I was,—and had but this fish painted, not a
holiday fool there but would give a piece of silver: there
would this monster make a man; any strange beast 30
there makes a man. When they will not give a doit to
relieve a lame beggar, they will lay out ten to see a dead
Indian. Legg'd like a man! and his fins like arms!
Warm, o' my troth! I do now let loose my opinion, hold
it no longer; this is no fish, but an islander, that hath 35
lately suffered by a thunderbolt. [*Thunder.*] Alas! the
storm is come again: my best way is to creep under his
gaberdine; there is no other shelter hereabout: misery
acquaints a man with strange bedfellows. I will here
shroud till the dregs of the storm be past.   40

   Enter STEPHANO, *singing; a bottle in his hand.*

Stephano. I shall no more to sea, to sea,
          Here shall I die a-shore:—

17 **mind**: notice.   18–19 **to bear off any weather**: to afford
any shelter.   20 **yond**: cf. I. ii. 406.   21 **bombard**: a large
leather vessel for holding wine.   27 **Poor-John**: salted hake.
28 **painted**: i.e. made into a picture. [*N*].   29 **holiday fool**: fool
on holiday.   30 **make**: make the fortune of.   31 **doit**: a small
Dutch coin, worth half a farthing.   33 **Legg'd**: with legs. (Trinculo
refers to Caliban.)   34 **o' my troth!**: upon my word!   38 **gaberdine**: a loose upper garment, a cloak.   40 **shroud**: shelter. [*N*].

This is a very scurvy tune to sing at a man's funeral:
Well, here's my comfort.   [*Drinks.*

The master, the swabber, the boatswain and I,   45
    The gunner and his mate,
Lov'd Mall, Meg, and Marian and Margery,
    But none of us car'd for Kate;
    For she had a tongue with a tang,
    Would cry to a sailor, 'Go hang!'   50
She lov'd not the savour of tar nor of pitch,
Yet a tailor might scratch her where-e'er she did itch:
    Then to sea, boys, and let her go hang.

This is a scurvy tune too: but here's my comfort. [*Drinks.*

  Caliban. Do not torment me: O!   55

  Stephano. What's the matter? Have we devils here?
Do you put tricks upon 's with salvages and men of
Ind? Ha! I have not 'scaped drowning, to be afeard
now of your four legs; for it hath been said, As proper
a man as ever went on four legs cannot make him give 60
ground: and it shall be said so again while Stephano
breathes at 'nostrils.

  Caliban. The spirit torments me: O!

  Stephano. This is some monster of the isle with four
legs, who hath got, as I take it, an ague. Where the 65
devil should he learn our language? I will give him
some relief, if it be but for that: if I can recover him and
keep him tame and get to Naples with him, he's a present for any emperor that ever trod on neat's-leather.

  Caliban. Do not torment me, prithee: I'll bring my wood
home faster.   71

  Stephano. He's in his fit now and does not talk after
the wisest. He shall taste of my bottle: if he have never

---

45 **swabber:** a sailor who cleans the decks.   57 **salvages:**
savages.   58 **Ind:** India. [*N*].   59–60 **As proper a man:** as
fine a fellow. [*N*].   62 **at 'nostrils:** at the nostrils, by the nose.
66 **should he learn:** can he have learnt.   67 **recover:** bring
about his recovery.   69 **neat's leather:** ox or cow hide.

drunk wine afore it will go near to remove his fit. If I
can recover him, and keep him tame, I will not take too   75
much for him: he shall pay for him that hath him, and
that soundly.

Caliban. Thou dost me yet but little hurt; thou wilt
anon, I know it by thy trembling: now Prosper works upon
thee.   80

Stephano. Come on your ways: open your mouth; here is
that which will give language to you, cat. Open your
mouth: this will shake your shaking, I can tell you, and
that soundly [*gives* CALIBAN *drink*]: you cannot tell who's
your friend; open your chaps again.   85

Trinculo. I should know that voice: it should be—but he
is drowned, and these are devils. O! defend me.

Stephano. Four legs and two voices; a most delicate
monster! His forward voice now is to speak well of his
friend; his backward voice is to utter foul speeches, and 90
to detract. If all the wine in my bottle will recover him,
I will help his ague. Come. Amen! I will pour some in
thy other mouth.

Trinculo. Stephano!   94

Stephano. Doth thy other mouth call me? Mercy! mercy!
This is a devil, and no monster: I will leave him; I have no
long spoon.

Trinculo. Stephano!—if thou beest Stephano, touch me,
and speak to me; for I am Trinculo:—be not afeard—thy
good friend Trinculo.   100

Stephano. If thou beest Trinculo, come forth. I'll pull
thee by the lesser legs: if any be Trinculo's legs, these are
they. Thou art very Trinculo indeed! How cam'st thou
to be the siege of this moon-calf? Can he vent Trinculos?

---

74 **afore**: before.   75–6 **I will not . . . him**: no price will
be too high for him, i.e. he's worth any money.   79 **anon**:
presently.   84–5 **you cannot . . . friend**: you don't know your
own friends.   85 **chaps**: jaws.   104 **siege**: excrement.

Trinculo. I took him to be killed with a thunder-stroke. 105
But art thou not drowned, Stephano? I hope now thou
art not drowned. Is the storm overblown? I hid me
under the dead moon-calf's gaberdine for fear of the
storm. And art thou living, Stephano? O Stephano!
two Neapolitans 'scaped! 110

Stephano. Prithee, do not turn me about: my stomach is
not constant.

Caliban. [*Aside.*] These be fine things an if they be not
sprites.
That's a brave god and bears celestial liquor:
I will kneel to him. 115

Stephano. How didst thou 'scape? How cam'st thou
hither? swear by this bottle, how thou cam'st hither. I
escaped upon a butt of sack, which the sailors heaved overboard, by this bottle! which I made of the bark of a tree
with mine own hands, since I was cast ashore. 120

Caliban. I'll swear upon that bottle, to be thy true subject; for the liquor is not earthly.

Stephano. Here: swear then, how thou escapedst.

Trinculo. Swam ashore, man, like a duck: I can swim like
a duck, I'll be sworn. 125

Stephano. Here, kiss the book [*gives* TRINCULO *drink*].
Though thou canst swim like a duck, thou art made like a
goose.

Trinculo. O Stephano! hast any more of this? 129

Stephano. The whole butt, man: my cellar is in a rock by
the seaside, where my wine is hid. How now, moon-calf!
how does thine ague?

Caliban. Hast thou not dropped from heaven?

Stephano. Out o' the moon, I do assure thee: I was the
man in the moon, when time was. 135

---

105 **him:** i.e. Stephano. 108 **moon-calf:** mis-shapen birth,
monster. 112 **constant:** firm, steady. 113 **an if:** if. 118 **sack:**
Spanish white wine. 135 **when time was:** once upon a time.

Caliban. I have seen thee in her, and I do adore thee; my mistress showed me thee, and thy dog, and thy bush.

Stephano. Come, swear to that; kiss the book; I will furnish it anon with new contents; swear.   139

Trinculo. By this good light, this is a very shallow monster.—I afeard of him!—a very weak monster.—The man i' the moon! a most poor credulous monster!—Well drawn, monster, in good sooth.

Caliban. I'll show thee every fertile inch o' the island; And I will kiss thy foot. I prithee, be my god.   145

Trinculo. By this light, a most perfidious and drunken monster: when his god's asleep, he'll rob his bottle.

Caliban. I'll kiss thy foot: I'll swear myself thy subject.

Stephano. Come on then; down, and swear.   149

Trinculo. I shall laugh myself to death at this puppy-headed monster. A most scurvy monster! I could find in my heart to beat him,—

Stephano. Come, kiss.

Trinculo. But that the poor monster's in drink: an abominable monster!   155

Caliban. I'll shew thee the best springs; I'll pluck thee berries;
I'll fish for thee, and get thee wood enough.
A plague upon the tyrant that I serve!
I'll bear him no more sticks, but follow thee,
Thou wondrous man.   160

Trinculo. A most ridiculous monster, to make a wonder of a poor drunkard!

Caliban. I prithee, let me bring thee where crabs grow;
And I with my long nails will dig thee pig-nuts;
Show thee a jay's nest and instruct thee how   165
To snare the nimble marmozet; I'll bring thee

142–3 **Well drawn**: you have taken a fine pull (draw) at the bottle.   154 **in drink**: intoxicated. [*N*].   163 **crabs**: crab-apples.   164 **pig-nuts**: earth-nuts, edible roots.

To clust'ring filberts, and sometimes I'll get thee
Young scamels from the rock. Wilt thou go with me?

Stephano. I prithee now, lead the way, without any more
talking.—Trinculo, the king and all our company else being
drowned, we will inherit here.—Here; bear my bottle.—
Fellow Trinculo, we'll fill him by and by again.   172

Caliban. Farewell, master; farewell, farewell.

                              [*Sings drunkenly.*
Trinculo. A howling monster, a drunken monster.

Caliban. No more dams I'll make for fish;   175
        Nor fetch in firing
        At requiring,
    Nor scrape trenchering, nor wash dish;
        'Ban, 'Ban, Ca—Caliban,
        Has a new master—Get a new man.   180

Freedom, high-day! high-day, freedom! freedom! high-
day, freedom!

Stephano. O brave monster! lead the way.   [*Exeunt.*

167 **filberts**: hazel nuts.   168 **scamels**: possibly 'sea-mews'.
[*N*].   170 **all our company else**: all the rest of our party.
171 **inherit**: enter into possession, dwell. [*N*].   177 **trenchering**:
Caliban's drunken rendering of trencher = a plate, or platter.
181 **high-day!** = hey-day!

ACT III

Scene I. BEFORE PROSPERO'S CELL

Enter FERDINAND, *bearing a log.*

Ferdinand. There be some sports are painful, and their
    labour
Delight in them sets off: some kinds of baseness
Are nobly undergone, and most poor matters
Point to rich ends. This my mean task
Would be as heavy to me as odious, but   5
The mistress which I serve quickens what's dead
And makes my labours pleasures: O! she is
Ten times more gentle than her father's crabbed,
And he's compos'd of harshness. I must remove
Some thousands of these logs and pile them up,   10
Upon a sore injunction: my sweet mistress
Weeps when she sees me work, and says such baseness
Had never like executor. I forget:
But these sweet thoughts do even refresh my labours,
Most busy lest when I do it.

Enter MIRANDA; *and* PROSPERO *behind.*

Miranda.   Alas! now, pray you   15
Work not so hard: I would the lightning had
Burnt up those logs that you are enjoined to pile!
Pray, set it down and rest you: when this burns,
'Twill weep for having wearied you. My father

    2 sets off: cancels. [*N*].   **most poor:** This is ambiguous.
Either (1) very trivial, or (2) the majority of trivial (matters).   5
but: but that.   **6 which:** archaic for 'whom'.   **quickens:**
makes quick (i.e. alive), gives life to.   **11 sore injunction:**
harsh order.   **12 baseness:** humble task.   **13 like executor:**
such a person performing (it).   **15 Most busy lest when I do
it:** i.e. busiest when I am least busy. [*N*].

Is hard at study; pray now, rest yourself: 20
He's safe for these three hours.

Ferdinand.   O most dear mistress,
The sun will set, before I shall discharge
What I must strive to do.

Miranda.   If you'll sit down,
I'll bear your logs the while. Pray, give me that;
I'll carry it to the pile.

Ferdinand.   No, precious creature: 25
I had rather crack my sinews, break my back,
Than you should such dishonour undergo,
While I sit lazy by.

Miranda.   It would become me
As well as it does you: and I should do it
With much more ease; for my good will is to it,   30
And yours it is against.

Prospero.   [*Aside.*] Poor worm! thou art infected:
This visitation shows it.

Miranda.   You look wearily.

Ferdinand. No, noble mistress; 'tis fresh morning with me
When you are by at night. I do beseech you—
Chiefly that I might set it in my prayers—   35
What is your name?

Miranda.   Miranda.—O my father!
I have broke your hest to say so.

Ferdinand.   Admir'd Miranda!
Indeed, the top of admiration; worth
What's dearest to the world! Full many a lady
I have ey'd with best regard, and many a time   40
The harmony of their tongues hath into bondage
Brought my too diligent ear: for several virtues
Have I lik'd several women; never any
With so full soul but some defect in her

37 **hest**: command. [*N*].   40 **best regard**: closest attention.
42 **several**: different.

Did quarrel with the noblest grace she ow'd,   45
And put it to the foil: but you, O you!
So perfect and so peerless, are created
Of every creature's best.
  Miranda.   I do not know
One of my sex; no woman's face remember,
Save, from my glass, mine own: nor have I seen   50
More that I may call men than you, good friend,
And my dear father: how features are abroad,
I am skill-less of; but, by my modesty,—
The jewel in my dower,—I would not wish
Any companion in the world but you;   55
Nor can imagination form a shape,
Besides yourself, to like of. But I prattle
Something too wildly and my father's precepts
I therein do forget.
  Ferdinand.   I am in my condition
A prince, Miranda; I do think, a king;—   60
I would not so!—and would no more endure
This wooden slavery than to suffer
The flesh-fly blow my mouth.—Hear my soul speak:—
The very instant that I saw you did
My heart fly to your service; there resides,   65
To make me slave to it; and for your sake
Am I this patient log-man.
  Miranda.   Do you love me?
  Ferdinand. O heaven! O earth! bear witness to this
     sound,
And crown what I profess with kind event

45 **ow'd:** possessed.   46 **put it to the foil:** defeated it.
48 **Of every creature's best:** out of the best features in all others.
53 **skill-less:** ignorant.   59 **condition:** worldly state.
61 **would no more endure:** i.e. if it were not for your sake. [*N*].
62 **wooden slavery:** the slavery of bearing logs.   63 **blow:**
literally, 'deposit its eggs in' (cf. 'fly-blown').   69 **kind
event:** prosperous result.

If I speak true: if hollowly, invert 70
What best is boded me to mischief! I,
Beyond all limit of what else i' the world,
Do love, prize, honour you.

Miranda. I am a fool
To weep at what I am glad of.

Prospero. [*Aside.*] Fair encounter
Of two most rare affections! Heavens rain grace 75
On that which breeds between 'em!

Ferdinand. Wherefore weep you?

Miranda. At mine unworthiness, that dare not offer
What I desire to give; and much less take
What I shall die to want. But this is trifling;
And all the more it seeks to hide itself 80
The bigger bulk it shows. Hence, bashful cunning!
And prompt me, plain and holy innocence!
I am your wife, if you will marry me;
If not, I'll die your maid: to be your fellow
You may deny me; but I'll be your servant 85
Whether you will or no.

Ferdinand. My mistress, dearest;
And I thus humble ever.

Miranda. My husband then?

Ferdinand. Ay, with a heart as willing
As bondage e'er of freedom: here's my hand.

Miranda. And mine, with my heart in 't: and now farewell 90
Till half an hour hence.

---

70 **hollowly:** falsely. 70–1 **invert . . . mischief!:**
turn all the best fortune that is promised me into evil. 72
what else: whatever else may be. 76 **that which breeds:**
i.e. their growing affection. 79 **to want:** for wanting,
i.e. for being without. 80 **it:** i.e. my love. 84
maid: unmarried girl. [*N*]. **fellow:** cf. II. i. 269. 89
As bondage e'er of freedom: as the prisoner is to be free
(of = for). [*N*].

Ferdinand.   A thousand thousand!

    [*Exeunt* FERDINAND *and* MIRANDA *severally.*

Prospero. So glad of this as they, I cannot be,
Who are surpris'd withal; but my rejoicing
At nothing can be more. I'll to my book;
For yet, ere supper time, must I perform   95
Much business appertaining.   [*Exit.*

Scene II. ANOTHER PART OF THE ISLAND

Enter CALIBAN, *with a bottle,* STEPHANO, *and* TRINCULO.

Stephano. Tell not me:—when the butt is out, we will
drink water; not a drop before: therefore bear up, and
board 'em.—Servant-monster, drink to me.

Trinculo. Servant-monster! the folly of this island! They
say there's but five upon this isle: we are three of them; if
th' other two be brained like us, the state totters.   6

Stephano. Drink, servant-monster, when I bid thee: thy
eyes are almost set in thy head.

Trinculo. Where should they be set else? he were a brave
monster indeed, if they were set in his tail.   10

Stephano. My man-monster hath drowned his tongue in
sack: for my part, the sea cannot drown me; I swam, ere
I could recover the shore, five-and-thirty leagues, off and
on, by this light. Thou shalt be my lieutenant, monster, or
my standard.   15

Trinculo. Your lieutenant, if you list; he's no standard.

Stephano. We'll not run, Monsieur monster.

Trinculo. Nor go neither: but you'll lie, like dogs; and
yet say nothing neither.

---

  93 **withal:** Either (1) in addition, as well, or (2) with it, at it. [*N*].
1 **out:** empty.   2 **bear up:** sail towards. [*N*].   6 **be
brained:** have brains.   9 **set:** fixed. [*N*].   13 **recover:**
reach.   15 **standard:** standard-bearer. [*N*].   18 **go:**
walk. **lie:** (1) lie down, (2) tell lies.

Stephano. Moon-calf, speak once in thy life, if thou beest
a good moon-calf.   21

Caliban. How does thy honour? Let me lick thy shoe.
I'll not serve him, he is not valiant.

Trinculo. Thou liest, most ignorant monster: I am in case
to justle a constable. Why, thou deboshed fish thou, was
there ever a man a coward that hath drunk so much sack as
I to-day? Wilt thou tell a monstrous lie, being but half a
fish and half a monster?

Caliban. Lo, how he mocks me! wilt thou let him, my
lord?   30

Trinculo. 'Lord' quoth he!—that a monster should be
such a natural!

Caliban. Lo, lo, again! bite him to death, I prithee.

Stephano. Trinculo, keep a good tongue in your head: if
you prove a mutineer, the next tree! The poor monster's
my subject, and he shall not suffer indignity.   36

Caliban. I thank my noble lord. Wilt thou be pleas'd
To hearken once again the suit I made thee?

Stephano. Marry, will I; kneel, and repeat it: I will stand,
and so shall Trinculo.   40

Enter ARIEL, *invisible.*

Caliban. As I told thee before, I am subject to a tyrant, a
sorcerer, that by his cunning hath cheated me of the island.

Ariel. Thou liest.

Caliban. Thou liest, thou jesting monkey thou; I would
my valiant master would destroy thee; I do not lie.   45

Stephano. Trinculo, if you trouble him any more in his
tale, by this hand, I will supplant some of your teeth.

24–5 **in case to:** in a condition to.   25 **deboshed:** besotted.
32 **natural:** simpleton.   35 **the next tree:** i.e. you will be
hanged on the nearest tree.   39 **Marry:** a mild oath ('by
Mary'), equivalent to 'By Jove!'   47 **supplant:** uproot.

Trinculo. Why, I said nothing.

Stephano. Mum then, and no more.—[*To* CALIBAN.] Proceed.   50

Caliban. I say, by sorcery he got this isle;
From me he got it: if thy greatness will
Revenge it on him,—for, I know, thou dar'st;
But this thing dare not,—

Stephano. That's most certain.   55

Caliban. Thou shalt be lord of it and I'll serve thee.

Stephano. How now shall this be compassed? Canst thou bring me to the party?

Caliban. Yea, yea, my lord: I'll yield him thee asleep,
Where thou may'st knock a nail into his head.   60

Ariel. Thou liest; thou canst not.

Caliban. What a pied ninny's this! Thou scurvy patch!—
I do beseech thy greatness, give him blows,
And take his bottle from him: when that's gone
He shall drink nought but brine; for I'll not show him   65
Where the quick freshes are.

Stephano. Trinculo, run into no further danger: interrupt the monster one word further, and, by this hand, I'll turn my mercy out o' doors and make a stock-fish of thee.

Trinculo. Why, what did I? I did nothing. I'll go further off.   71

Stephano. Didst thou not say he lied?

Ariel. Thou liest.

Stephano. Do I so? take thou that. [*Strikes* TRINCULO.]
As you like this, give me the lie another time.   75

Trinculo. I did not give thee the lie:—Out o' your wits

---

49 **Mum:** silence!   52 **thy greatness:** i.e. your lordship.
54 **this thing:** i.e. Trinculo.   58 **the party:** the person concerned. [*N*].   59 **yield him thee:** give him up to you.   62
pied ninny: motley fool. [*N*].   **patch:** clown.   66 **quick freshes:** flowing springs, or streams.   69 **stock-fish:** dried and salted cod. [*N*].   75 **give me the lie:** contradict me.

and hearing too?—A pox o' your bottle! this can sack and
drinking do.—A murrain on your monster, and the devil
take your fingers!

Caliban. Ha, ha, ha! 80

Stephano. Now, forward with your tale.—Prithee stand
further off.

Caliban. Beat him enough: after a little time
I'll beat him too.

Stephano. Stand further.—Come, proceed.

Caliban. Why, as I told thee, 'tis a custom with him 85
I' the afternoon to sleep: there thou may'st brain him,
Having first seized his books; or with a log
Batter his skull, or paunch him with a stake,
Or cut his wezand with thy knife. Remember
First to possess his books; for without them 90
He's but a sot, as I am, nor hath not
One spirit to command: they all do hate him
As rootedly as I. Burn but his books;
He has brave utensils,—for so he calls them,—
Which, when he has a house, he'll deck withal: 95
And that most deeply to consider is
The beauty of his daughter; he himself
Calls her a nonpareil: I never saw a woman,
But only Sycorax my dam and she;
But she as far surpasseth Sycorax 100
As great'st does least.

Stephano. Is it so brave a lass?

Caliban. Ay, lord; she will become thy bed, I warrant,
And bring thee forth brave brood.

78 murrain: a (cattle) disease. **88 paunch:** stab in the
stomach. **89 wezand:** wind-pipe. **90 possess:** get
possession of. **91 sot:** blockhead. **93 but:** only. **94
brave:** cf. I. ii. 6, &c. [N]. **95 Which . . . withal:** with
which he will adorn his house when he has one. **96 that
most deeply to consider:** the thing most worth considering, the
greatest attraction.

Stephano. Monster, I will kill this man: his daughter and I will be king and queen,—save our graces! and Trinculo and thyself shall be viceroys. Dost thou like the plot, Trinculo?   107

Trinculo. Excellent.

Stephano. Give me thy hand: I am sorry I beat thee; but, while thou livest, keep a good tongue in thy head.   110

Caliban. Within this half hour will he be asleep;
Wilt thou destroy him then?

Stephano.   Ay, on mine honour.

Ariel. This will I tell my master.

Caliban. Thou mak'st me merry: I am full of pleasure.
Let us be jocund: will you troll the catch   115
You taught me but while-ere?

Stephano. At thy request, monster, I will do reason, any reason: Come on, Trinculo, let us sing.   [*Sings.*

Flout 'em, and scout 'em; and scout 'em, and flout 'em;
Thought is free.   120

Caliban. That's not the tune.

               [ARIEL *plays the tune on a Tabor and Pipe.*

Stephano. What is this same?

Trinculo. This is the tune of our catch, played by the picture of Nobody.

Stephano. If thou beest a man, show thyself in thy likeness: if thou beest a devil, take 't as thou list.   126

Trinculo. O, forgive me my sins!

Stephano. He that dies pays all debts: I defy thee.
—Mercy upon us!

Caliban. Art thou afeard?   130

Stephano. No, monster, not I.

---

105 **save:** cf. II. i. 165.   115 **troll the catch:** sing the part-song. [*N*].   116 **but while-ere:** only a short time ago.   117 **do reason:** give you satisfaction. [*N*].   (*s.d.*) *Tabor*: a small drum carried at the side.   126 **as thou list:** as you like. [*N*].

✓ *Caliban.* Be not afeard: the isle is full of noises,
Sounds and sweet airs, that give delight, and hurt not.
Sometimes a thousand twangling instruments
Will hum about mine ears; and sometime voices,   135
That, if I then had wak'd after long sleep,
Will make me sleep again: and then, in dreaming,
The clouds methought would open and show riches
Ready to drop upon me; that, when I wak'd
I cried to dream again.   140
    Stephano. This will prove a brave kingdom to me, where
I shall have my music for nothing.
    Caliban. When Prospero is destroyed.
    Stephano. That shall be by and by: I remember the story.
    Trinculo. The sound is going away: let's follow it, and
after do our work.   146
    Stephano. Lead, monster; we'll follow.—I would I could
see this taborer! he lays it on.
    Trinculo. Wilt come? I'll follow Stephano.   [*Exeunt.*

Scene III. ANOTHER PART OF THE ISLAND

Enter ALONSO, SEBASTIAN, ANTONIO, GONZALO, ADRIAN,
FRANCISCO, *and others.*

    Gonzalo. By'r lakin, I can go no further, sir;
My old bones ache: here's a maze trod indeed,
Through forth-rights, and meanders! by your patience,
I needs must rest me.
    Alonso.   Old lord, I cannot blame thee,
Who am myself attach'd with weariness,   5

---

144 **by and by**: immediately (cf. 'presently'). [*N*].   148 **he lays
it on**: he thumps his drum vigorously.   1 **By'r lakin**: by our
ladykin (i.e. little Lady, viz. the Virgin Mary).   3 **forth-rights**:
straight paths. **meanders**: wandering paths. **by your patience**:
with your leave.   5 **attach'd**: seized.

To the dulling of my spirits: sit down, and rest.
Even here I will put off my hope, and keep it
No longer for my flatterer: he is drown'd
Whom thus we stray to find; and the sea mocks
Our frustrate search on land. Well, let him go.   10
   Antonio. [*Aside to* SEBASTIAN.] I am right glad that he's
     so out of hope.
Do not, for one repulse, forego the purpose
That you resolv'd to effect.
   Sebastian. [*Aside to* ANTONIO.] The next advantage
Will we take throughly.
   Antonio. [*Aside to* SEBASTIAN.] Let it be to-night;
For, now they are oppress'd with travel, they   15
Will not, nor cannot, use such vigilance
As when they are fresh.
   Sebastian. [*Aside to* ANTONIO.] I say to-night: no more.

> *Solemn and strange music; and* PROSPERO *on the top,
> invisible. Enter several strange Shapes, bringing in a
> banquet, and dance about it with gentle actions of saluta-
> tion; and, inviting the King, &c., to eat, they depart.*

   Alonso. What harmony is this? my good friends, hark!
   Gonzalo. Marvellous sweet music!
   Alonso. Give us kind keepers, heavens! What were these?
   Sebastian. A living drollery. Now I will believe   21
That there are unicorns; that in Arabia
There is one tree, the phoenix' throne; one phoenix
At this hour reigning there.
   Antonio.   I'll believe both;
And what does else want credit, come to me,   25

---

  6 **To the dulling . . . spirits**: to such an extent that my spirits
are dulled.   8 **for my flatterer**: to be my flatterer, to flatter me.
10 **frustrate**: vain, unavailing.   13 **advantage**: opportunity.
14 **throughly**: thoroughly.   20 **keepers**: guardian angels.
21 **drollery**: puppet-show.   25 **want credit**: fail to gain belief.
25 **come to me**: come and ask me about it.

And I'll be sworn 'tis true: travellers ne'er did lie,
Though fools at home condemn them.

Gonzalo.   If in Naples
I should report this now, would they believe me?
If I should say I saw such islanders,—
For, certes, these are people of the island,—   30
Who, though they are of monstrous shape, yet, note,
Their manners are more gentle-kind than of
Our human generation you shall find
Many, nay, almost any.

Prospero.   [*Aside.*] Honest lord,
Thou hast said well; for some of you there present   35
Are worse than devils.

Alonso.   I cannot too much muse
Such shapes, such gesture, and such sound, expressing,—
Although they want the use of tongue,—a kind
Of excellent dumb discourse.

Prospero.   [*Aside.*] Praise in departing.

Francisco. They vanish'd strangely.

Sebastian.   No matter, since   40
They have left their viands behind; for we have stomachs.—
Will't please you to taste of what is here?

Alonso.   Not I.

Gon. Faith, sir, you need not fear. When we were boys,
Who would believe that there were mountaineers
Dew-lapp'd like bulls, whose throats had hanging at
    them   45
Wallets of flesh? or that there were such men
Whose heads stood in their breasts? which now we find
Each putter-out of five for one will bring us

30 **certes:** truly.   32 **gentle-kind:** courteous. [*N*].   33
generation: race, birth.   36 **muse:** marvel at.   39
Praise in departing: Be careful how you praise! [*N*].   48 **Each
putter-out of five for one:** each traveller (who has taken out an
insurance on his safe return). [*N*].

Good warrant of.

   Alonso.   I will stand to and feed,
Although my last; no matter, since I feel   **50**
The best is past.—Brother, my lord the duke,
Stand to and do as we.

> *Thunder and lightning. Enter* ARIEL *like a harpy; claps
> his wings upon the table; and, with a quaint device, the
> banquet vanishes.*

   Ariel. You are three men of sin, whom Destiny—
That hath to instrument this lower world
And what is in't,—the never-surfeited sea   **55**
Hath caused to belch up you; and on this island
Where man doth not inhabit; you 'mongst men
Being most unfit to live. I have made you mad;
> [*Seeing* ALONSO, SEBASTIAN, *&c., draw their swords.*
And even with such-like valour men hang and drown
Their proper selves. You fools! I and my fellows   **60**
Are ministers of fate: the elements
Of whom your swords are temper'd, may as well
Wound the loud winds, or with bemock'd-at stabs
Kill the still-closing waters, as diminish
One dowle that's in my plume; my fellow-ministers   **65**
Are like invulnerable. If you could hurt,
Your swords are now too massy for your strengths,

---

   49 stand to: fall to, i.e. begin to eat. [*N*].   **50 Although my
last:** i.e. although my last meal, if it is the last food I ever eat.
51 The best: i.e. the best part of my life.   **54 to instrument:**
as its (i.e. Destiny's) instrument.   **55–6 the never-surfeited
. . . up you:** (whom Destiny) has caused the ever-hungry sea to
vomit up. [*N*].   **57 inhabit:** dwell.   **57–8 you . . .
Being:** seeing that you are.   **60 Their proper selves:** their
own essential selves, their true nature.   **61 ministers:** servants
(cf. I. ii. 131).   **62 whom:** which. [*N*].   **64 still-closing:**
constantly closing (cf. 'still-vex'd', I. ii. 229).   **65 dowle:** down
feather.   **66 like:** equally, in like manner.   **67 massy:** heavy.

And will not be uplifted. But, remember,—
For that's my business to you,—that you three
From Milan did supplant good Prospero; 70
Expos'd unto the sea, which hath requit it,
Him and his innocent child: for which foul deed
The powers, delaying, not forgetting, have
Incens'd the seas and shores, yea, all the creatures,
Against your peace. Thee of thy son, Alonso, 75
They have bereft; and do pronounce, by me,
Lingering perdition,—worse than any death
Can be at once,—shall step by step attend
You and your ways; whose wraths to guard you from—
Which here in this most desolate isle, else falls 80
Upon your heads,—is nothing but heart-sorrow
And a clear life ensuing.

> *He vanishes in thunder: then, to soft music, enter the*
> *Shapes again, and dance with mocks and mows, and*
> *carrying out the table.*

Prospero. [*Aside.*] Bravely the figure of this harpy hast
thou
Perform'd, my Ariel; a grace it had, devouring:
Of my instruction hast thou nothing bated 85
In what thou hadst to say: so, with good life
And observation strange, my meaner ministers
Their several kinds have done. My high charms work,
And these mine enemies are all knit up

71 **requit**: requited.   74 **all the creatures**: all creation.
76 **pronounce**: pronounce (that).   79 **whose**: i.e. of the powers
(l. 73).   81 **is nothing but**: i.e. there is nothing for it, no alternative, but.   82 **clear**: blameless.   (*s.d.*) *mows*: grimaces.
84 **devouring**: absorbing. [*N*].   85 **bated**: omitted.   86
good life: with great liveliness. [*N*].   87 **observation**: obser-
vant care.   **strange**: unusual, exceptional.   88 **Their several
kinds**: according to their several natures.   **high**: strong, powerful.
89 **knit up**: tied up, bound.

In their distractions: they now are in my power;   90
And in these fits I leave them, while I visit
Young Ferdinand,—whom they suppose is drown'd,—
And his and mine lov'd darling.   [*Exit above.*

  Gon. I' the name of something holy, sir, why stand you
In this strange stare?

  Alonso.   O, it is monstrous! monstrous!   95
Methought the billows spoke and told me of it;
The winds did sing it to me; and the thunder,
That deep and dreadful organ-pipe, pronounc'd
The name of Prosper: it did bass my trespass.
Therefore my son i' th' ooze is bedded; and   100
I'll seek him deeper than e'er plummet sounded,
And with him there lie mudded.   [*Exit.*

  Sebastian.   But one fiend at a time,
I'll fight their legions o'er.

  Antonio.   I'll be thy second.

             [*Exeunt* SEBASTIAN *and* ANTONIO.

  Gonzalo. All three of them are desperate; their great guilt,
Like poison given to work a great time after,   105
Now 'gins to bite the spirits.—I do beseech you
That are of suppler joints, follow them swiftly
And hinder them from what this ecstasy
May now provoke them to.

  Adrian.   Follow, I pray you.   [*Exeunt.*

---

  96 it: i.e. Alonso's fault.   **99 it did bass my trespass:** it
told my fault in a deep voice.   **102 mudded:** buried in mud.
102–3. But one . . . o'er: provided I can take on the fiends one at
a time, I'll fight them all.   **105 given . . . after:** administered
with the intention that it should take effect much later (or, 'given
to'='whose nature it is to').   **106 'gins:** begins.   **108 ecstasy:**
frenzy.

ACT IV

Scene I. BEFORE PROSPERO'S CELL

Enter PROSPERO, FERDINAND, *and* MIRANDA.

Prospero. If I have too austerely punish'd you,
Your compensation makes amends; for I
Have given you here a third of mine own life,
Or that for which I live; whom once again
I tender to thy hand: all thy vexations   5
Were but my trials of thy love, and thou
Hast strangely stood the test: here, afore Heaven,
I ratify this my rich gift. O Ferdinand!
Do not smile at me that I boast her off,
For thou shalt find she will outstrip all praise,   10
And make it halt behind her.
   Ferdinand.   I do believe it
Against an oracle.
   Prospero. Then, as my gift and thine own acquisition
Worthily purchas'd, take my daughter: but
If thou dost break her virgin knot before   15
All sanctimonious ceremonies may
With full and holy rite be minister'd,
No sweet aspersion shall the heavens let fall
To make this contract grow; but barren hate,
Sour-ey'd disdain and discord shall bestrew   20
The union of your bed with weeds so loathly
That you shall hate it both: therefore take heed,

7 strangely: wonderfully.   **afore:** before.   **9 boast her off:** speak with pride of her. [*N*].   **11 halt:** limp (verb).   **12 Against an oracle:** i.e. if an oracle were to pronounce differently. **14 purchas'd:** acquired.   **15 break her virgin knot:** treat her as your wife.   **16 sanctimonious:** holy.   **18 aspersion:** that which is sprinkled, a shower. [*N*].   **22 you ... both:** both of you.

As Hymen's lamps shall light you.

Ferdinand.   As I hope
For quiet days, fair issue and long life,
With such love as 'tis now, the murkiest den,   25
The most opportune place, the strong'st suggestion
Our worser genius can, shall never melt
Mine honour into lust, to take away
The edge of that day's celebration
When I shall think, or Phoebus' steeds are founder'd,   30
Or Night kept chain'd below.

Prospero.   Fairly spoke:
Sit then, and talk with her, she is thine own.
What, Ariel! my industrious servant Ariel!

Enter ARIEL.

Ariel. What would my potent master? here I am.

Prospero. Thou and thy meaner fellows your last service
Did worthily perform; and I must use you   36
In such another trick. Go bring the rabble,
O'er whom I give thee power, here to this place:
Incite them to quick motion; for I must
Bestow upon the eyes of this young couple   40
Some vanity of mine art: it is my promise,
And they expect it from me.

Ariel.   Presently?

Prospero. Ay, with a twink.

Ariel. Before you can say, 'Come,' and 'Go,'
And breathe twice; and cry, 'so, so,'   45

23 **As**: in such a way that. [*N*].   24 **issue**: progeny, children.
25 **as 'tis now**: i.e. as my love now is.   26 **opportune**: convenient, fitting the circumstances (accent 'oppórtune'). **suggestion**:
temptation.   27 **can**: i.e. can make.   28 **to take**: i.e. so
as to take. [*N*].   30 **founder'd**: gone lame. [*N*].   33 **What,
Ariel!**: Hullo there, Ariel! [*N*].   41 **vanity**: illusion (or, perhaps,
'trifle').   42 **Presently**: at once.   43 **with a twink**: in a
twinkle.

Each one, tripping on his toe,
Will be here with mop and mow.
Do you love me, master? no?

   Prospero. Dearly, my delicate Ariel. Do not approach
Till thou dost hear me call.

   Ariel.   Well: I conceive.   [*Exit.* 50

   Prospero. [*To* FERDINAND.] Look thou be true; do not
      give dalliance
Too much the rein: the strongest oaths are straw
To the fire i' the blood: be more abstemious,
Or else good night your vow!

   Ferdinand.   I warrant you, sir;
The white-cold virgin snow upon my heart   55
Abates the ardour of my liver.

   Prospero.   Well.—
Now come, my Ariel! bring a corollary,
Rather than want a spirit: appear, and pertly.
No tongue! all eyes! be silent.   [*Soft music.*

         A Masque. Enter IRIS.

   Iris. Ceres, most bounteous lady, thy rich leas   60
Of wheat, rye, barley, vetches, oats, and peas;
Thy turfy mountains, where live nibbling sheep,
And flat meads thatch'd with stover, them to keep;
Thy banks with pioned and twilled brims,
Which spongy April at thy hest betrims,   65
To make cold nymphs chaste crowns; and thy broom
      groves,

---

   47 mop and mow: grimaces.   **50 Well:** it is well; good!
conceive: understand.   **54 good night your vow!:** it will be
the end of your vow!   **55 The white-cold . . . snow:** i.e.
Miranda's pure breast.   **56 Well:** cf. l. 50. [*N*].   **57 corollary:**
a surplus, too many.   **58 pertly:** promptly.   **60 leas:**
arable land. [*N*].   **63 stover:** cattle fodder.   **64 pioned and**
twilled: trenched and ridged (?) [*N*].   **65 spongy:** showery.

+plant of bean family used for fodder.

Whose shadow the dismissed bachelor loves,
Being lass-lorn; thy pole-clipt vineyard;
And thy sea-marge, sterile and rocky-hard,
Where thou thyself dost air: the queen o' the sky,   70
Whose watery arch and messenger am I,
Bids thee leave these; and with her sovereign grace.
Here on this grass-plot, in this very place,
To come and sport; her peacocks fly amain:
Approach, rich Ceres, her to entertain.   75

Enter CERES.

Ceres. Hail, many-colour'd messenger, that ne'er
Dost disobey the wife of Jupiter;
Who with thy saffron wings upon my flowers
Diffusest honey-drops, refreshing showers:
And with each end of thy blue bow dost crown   80
My bosky acres, and my unshrubb'd down,
Rich scarf to my proud earth; why hath thy queen
Summon'd me hither, to this short-grass'd green?
Iris. A contract of true love to celebrate,
And some donation freely to estate   85
On the bless'd lovers.
Ceres.   Tell me, heavenly bow,
If Venus or her son, as thou dost know,
Do now attend the queen? since they did plot
The means that dusky Dis my daughter got,
Her and her blind boy's scandal'd company   90

---

67 **dismissed**: rejected.   68 **pole-clipt**: with poles clasped
(by vines).   70 **queen o' the sky**: Juno.   72 **her sovereign
grace**: i.e. her Majesty.   74 **amain**: swiftly. [*N*].   79 **honey-
drops**: honey dew. [*N*].   80 **blue bow**: i.e. the rainbow.
81 **bosky**: wooded.   **unshrubb'd**: bare of shrubs.   82 **proud**:
splendid, magnificent. [*N*].   85 **estate**: give as an estate,
bestow. [*N*].   87 **her son**: i.e. Cupid.   89 **that**: by which.
Dis: Pluto. [*N*].   90 **scandal'd**: disgraced, shameful.

I have forsworn.
    Iris.   Of her society
Be not afraid; I met her deity
Cutting the clouds towards Paphos and her son
Dove-drawn with her. Here thought they to have done
Some wanton charm upon this man and maid,   95
Whose vows are, that no bed-rite shall be paid
Till Hymen's torch be lighted; but in vain:
Mars's hot minion is return'd again;
Her waspish-headed son has broke his arrows,
Swears he will shoot no more, but play with sparrows,   100
And be a boy right out.
    Ceres.   Highest queen of state,
Great Juno comes; I know her by her gait.

JUNO *descends.*

Juno. How does my bounteous sister? Go with me
To bless this twain, that they may prosperous be,
And honour'd in their issue.   105

SONG

Juno. Honour, riches, marriage-blessing,
       Long continuance, and increasing,
       Hourly joys be still upon you!
       Juno sings her blessings on you.

Ceres. Earth's increase, foison plenty,   110
       Barns and garners never empty:
       Vines, with clust'ring bunches growing;
       Plants with goodly burden bowing;

  92 her deity: her godship, i.e. Venus.   **93 Cutting the
clouds**: cleaving the sky. [*N*].   **98 hot minion**: wanton darling
(i.e. Venus).   **101 a boy right out**: an out-and-out, real boy.
110 foison: abundance (cf. II. i. 160).

Spring come to you at the farthest
In the very end of harvest!   115
Scarcity and want shall shun you;
Ceres' blessing so is on you.

   Ferdinand. This is a most majestic vision, and
Harmonious charmingly: May I be bold
To think these spirits?
   Prospero.   Spirits, which by mine art   120
I have from their confines call'd to enact
My present fancies.
   Ferdinand.   Let me live here ever:
So rare a wonder'd father and a wise,
Makes this place Paradise.

                [JUNO *and* CERES *whisper, and send* IRIS *on*
                                     employment.
   Prospero.   Sweet, now, silence!
Juno and Ceres whisper seriously,   125
There's something else to do: hush, and be mute,
Or else our spell is marr'd.
   Iris. You nymphs, call'd Naiades, of the windring brooks,
With your sedg'd crowns, and ever-harmless looks,
Leave your crisp channels, and on this green land   130
Answer your summons: Juno does command.
Come, temperate nymphs, and help to celebrate
A contract of true love: be not too late.

Enter certain Nymphs.

You sun-burn'd sicklemen, of August weary,
Come hither from the furrow, and be merry: 135

   114 farthest: latest. [*N*].   **117 so:** to that end.   121
confines: *Either* (1) places of confinement, *or* (2) territories.   123
rare: remarkable. **wonder'd:** performing wonders. 128 **win-**
dring: winding. [*N*].   129 **sedg'd:** reedy.   130 **crisp:**
rippled.   **land:** possibly a variant of 'laund' = glade.   135
furrow: here equivalent to 'cornfields'.

Make holiday: your rye-straw hats put on,
And these fresh nymphs encounter every one
In country footing.

> *Enter certain* Reapers, *properly habited: they join with
> the* Nymphs *in a graceful dance; towards the end whereof*
> PROSPERO *starts suddenly, and speaks; after which, to a
> strange, hollow, and confused noise, they heavily vanish.*

Prospero. [*Aside.*] I had forgot that foul conspiracy
Of the beast Caliban, and his confederates   140
Against my life: the minute of their plot
Is almost come.—[*To the* Spirits.] Well done! avoid; no
    more!
Ferdinand. This is strange: your father's in some
    passion
That works him strongly.
Miranda.   Never till this day
Saw I him touch'd with anger so distemper'd.   145
Prospero. You do look, my son, in a mov'd sort,
As if you were dismay'd: be cheerful, sir:
Our revels now are ended. These our actors,
As I foretold you, were all spirits and
Are melted into air, into thin air: 150
And, like the baseless fabric of this vision,
The cloud-capp'd towers, the gorgeous palaces,
The solemn temples, the great globe itself,
Yea, all which it inherit, shall dissolve
And, like this insubstantial pageant faded,   155
Leave not a rack behind. We are such stuff

138 **footing:** dancing.   (*s.d.*) *properly habited*: dressed as
reapers would naturally be dressed.   142 **avoid:** begone.
143 **passion:** strong emotion.   144 **works:** agitates.   145
distemper'd: immoderate, violent.   146 **You do look . . . in
a mov'd sort:** you seem to be deeply stirred.   154 **it inherit:**
occupy, possess it.   156 **rack:** driving mist or fog.

As dreams are made on, and our little life
Is rounded with a sleep.—Sir, I am vex'd:
Bear with my weakness; my old brain is troubled.
Be not disturb'd with my infirmity.   160
If you be pleas'd, retire into my cell
And there repose: a turn or two I'll walk,
To still my beating mind.
    Ferdinand.   *Miranda.*   We wish your peace.   [*Exeunt.*
    Pro. Come with a thought!—I thank thee, Ariel; come!

Enter ARIEL.

    Ariel. Thy thoughts I cleave to. What's thy pleasure?
    Prospero.   Spirit,   165
We must prepare to meet with Caliban.
    Ariel. Ay, my commander; when I presented Ceres,
I thought to have told thee of it; but I fear'd
Lest I might anger thee.   169
    Pro. Say again, where didst thou leave these varlets?
    Ariel. I told you, sir, they were red-hot with drinking;
So full of valour that they smote the air
For breathing in their faces; beat the ground
For kissing of their feet; yet always bending
Towards their project. Then I beat my tabor;   175
At which, like unback'd colts, they prick'd their ears,
Advanc'd their eyelids, lifted up their noses
As they smelt music: so I charm'd their ears
That, calf-like, they my lowing follow'd through
Tooth'd briers, sharp furzes, pricking goss and thorns,   180
Which enter'd their frail shins: at last I left them
I' the filthy-mantled pool beyond your cell,

    157 on: of (cf. i. ii. 87).   **163 beating**: agitated.   **166
meet with**: encounter.   **167 presented**: represented, played
the part of.   **170 varlets**: rogues.   **174 bending**: proceeding.
176 unback'd: unbroken, never yet ridden.   **178 As**: as if.
180 goss: gorse.   **182 filthy-mantled**: covered with filthy scum.

There dancing up to the chins, that the foul lake
O'erstunk their feet.

   Prospero.   This was well done, my bird.
Thy shape invisible retain thou still: 185
The trumpery in my house, go bring it hither,
For stale to catch these thieves.

   Ariel.   I go, I go.   [*Exit.*
   Prospero. A devil, a born devil, on whose nature
Nurture can never stick; on whom my pains,
Humanely taken, are all lost, quite lost;   190
And as with age his body uglier grows,
So his mind cankers. I will plague them all,
Even to roaring.

   Re-enter ARIEL, *loaden with glistering apparel, &c.*

          Come, hang them on this line. *lime*

   PROSPERO *and* ARIEL *remain invisible.* Enter CALIBAN,
STEPHANO, *and* TRINCULO, *all wet.*

   Caliban. Pray you, tread softly, that the blind mole may
    not
Hear a foot fall: we now are near his cell.   195
   Stephano. Monster, your fairy, which you say is a harmless
fairy, has done little better than played the Jack with us.
   Trinculo. Monster, I do smell all horse-piss; at which my
nose is in great indignation.
   Stephano. So is mine.—Do you hear, monster? If I
should take a displeasure against you, look you,—   201
   Trinculo. Thou wert but a lost monster.
   Caliban. Good my lord, give me thy favour still:

---

184 **O'erstunk**: stank worse than. [*N*].   187 **stale**: decoy,
bait. [*N*].   188 **A devil**: i.e. Caliban is a devil.   189 **Nurture**:
education.   193 **to roaring**: till they roar.   **line**: *either* 'lime-
tree', *or* 'clothes-line'. [*N*].   196 **fairy**: i.e. Ariel.   197
played the Jack: played the knave, tricked.

Be patient, for the prize I'll bring thee to
Shall hoodwink this mischance: therefore speak softly; 205
All's hush'd as midnight yet.

Trinculo. Ay, but to lose our bottles in the pool,—

Stephano. There is not only disgrace and dishonour in
that, monster, but an infinite loss.

Trinculo. That's more to me than my wetting: yet this is
your harmless fairy, monster.   211

Stephano. I will fetch off my bottle, though I be o'er ears
for my labour.

Caliban. Prithee, my king, be quiet. Seest thou here,
This is the mouth o' the cell: no noise, and enter.   215
Do that good mischief, which may make this island
Thine own for ever, and I, thy Caliban,
For aye thy foot-licker.

Stephano. Give me thy hand: I do begin to have bloody
thoughts.   220

Trinculo. O king Stephano! O peer! O worthy Stephano!
look, what a wardrobe here is for thee!

Caliban. Let it alone, thou fool; it is but trash.

Trinculo. O, ho, monster! we know what belongs to a
frippery.—O king Stephano!   225

Stephano. Put off that gown, Trinculo; by this hand, I'll
have that gown.

Trinculo. Thy grace shall have it.

Caliban. The dropsy drown this fool! what do you
    mean
To dote thus on such luggage? Let's along,   230
And do the murder first: if he awake,
From toe to crown he'll fill our skins with pinches;
Make us strange stuff.

Stephano. Be you quiet, monster.—Mistress line, is not

---

205 **hoodwink this mischance:** hide this unfortunate event
from our eyes, i.e. make it as if it had never happened. [*N*].   225
frippery: old clothes shop.   230 **luggage:** goods.

this my jerkin? Now is the jerkin under the line: now,
jerkin, you are like to lose your hair and prove a bald jerkin.

Trinculo. Do, do: we steal by line and level, an 't like
your grace.   238

Stephano. I thank thee for that jest; here's a garment
for 't: wit shall not go unrewarded while I am king of
this country: 'Steal by line and level,' is an excellent pass
of pate; there's another garment for 't.

Trinculo. Monster, come, put some lime upon your fingers,
and away with the rest.   244

Caliban. I will have none on 't: we shall lose our time,
And all be turned to barnacles, or to apes
With foreheads villanous low.

Stephano. Monster, lay-to your fingers: help to bear this
away where my hogshead of wine is, or I'll turn you out of
my kingdom. Go to; carry this.   250

Trinculo. And this.

Stephano. Ay, and this.

> *A noise of hunters heard. Enter divers* Spirits, *in shape
> of hounds, and hunt them about;* PROSPERO *and* ARIEL
> *setting them on.*

Prospero. Hey, Mountain, hey!

Ariel. Silver! there it goes, Silver!

Prospero. Fury, Fury! there, Tyrant, there! hark, hark!

> [CALIBAN, STEPHANO, *and* TRINCULO *are driven out.*

Go, charge my goblins that they grind their joints   256
With dry convulsions; shorten up their sinews
With aged cramps, and more pinch-spotted make them
Than pard, or cat o' mountain.

237 **by line and level:** methodically.   **an 't like:** if it please.
241–2 **pass of pate:** sally of wit. [*N*].   243 **lime:** bird-lime. [*N*].
246 **barnacles:** wild geese. [*N*].   248 **lay-to:** bring to bear.
258 **aged cramps:** cramps such as attack the very old.   258–9
more pinch-spotted . . . mountain: give them more spots (from
pinching) than there are on a leopard or wild cat.

Ariel.   Hark! they roar.

Prospero. Let them be hunted soundly. At this hour 260
Lie at my mercy all mine enemies:
Shortly shall all my labours end, and thou
Shalt have the air at freedom: for a little,
Follow, and do me service.   [*Exeunt.*

263 **at freedom:** at liberty, as a free person.

ACT V

Scene I. BEFORE THE CELL OF PROSPERO

Enter PROSPERO *in his magic robes; and* ARIEL.

Prospero. Now does my project gather to a head:
My charms crack not; my spirits obey, and time *[time is keeping pace with events]*
Goes upright with his carriage. How's the day?

Ariel. On the sixth hour; at which time, my lord,
You said our work should cease.

Prospero.   I did say so,   5
When first I rais'd the tempest. Say, my spirit,
How fares the king and 's followers?

Ariel.   Confin'd together
In the same fashion as you gave in charge;
Just as you left them: all prisoners, sir,
In the line-grove which weather-fends your cell;   10
They cannot budge till your release. The king,
His brother, and yours, abide all three distracted,
And the remainder mourning over them,
Brimful of sorrow and dismay; but chiefly
Him, that you term'd, sir, 'The good old lord Gonzalo:' 15
His tears run down his beard, like winter's drops
From eaves of reeds; your charm so strongly works
      them,
That if you now beheld them, your affections
Would become tender.

Prospero.   Dost thou think so, spirit?

Ariel. Mine would, sir, were I human.

Prospero.   And mine shall. 20

3 carriage: what he is carrying. [*N*].   **8 gave in charge:**
commanded.   **10 weather-fends:** shelters from the weather.
11 till your release: i.e. till you release them.   **12 abide:**
continue to be.   **17 works:** moves, affects (cf. IV. i. 144).

Hast thou, which art but air, a touch, a feeling
Of their afflictions, and shall not myself,
One of their kind, that relish all as sharply,
Passion as they, be kindlier mov'd than thou art?
Though with their high wrongs I am struck to the quick, 25
Yet with my nobler reason 'gainst my fury
Do I take part: the rarer action is
In virtue than in vengeance: they being penitent,
The sole drift of my purpose doth extend
Not a frown further. Go, release them, Ariel.   30
My charms I'll break, their senses I'll restore,
And they shall be themselves.

    Ariel.   I'll fetch them, sir. [*Exit.*
    Prospero. Ye elves of hills, brooks, standing lakes, and
        groves;
And ye, that on the sands with printless foot
Do chase the ebbing Neptune and do fly him   35
When he comes back; you demi-puppets, that
By moonshine do the green sour ringlets make
Whereof the ewe not bites; and you, whose pastime
Is to make midnight mushrumps; that rejoice
To hear the solemn curfew; by whose aid,—   40
Weak masters though ye be—I have bedimm'd
The noontide sun, call'd forth the mutinous winds,
And 'twixt the green sea and the azur'd vault
Set roaring war: to the dread-rattling thunder
Have I given fire and rifted Jove's stout oak   45

21 **touch**: sensibility.   23 **that relish all as sharply**: who
feel (literally 'taste') just as keenly.   24 **Passion**: feel suffering. [*N*].   25 **their high wrongs**: the deep wrongs done by them.
27 **rarer**: finer, nobler. [*N*].   29 **The sole drift of my purpose**: my intentions which have been directed exclusively to one
end.   30 **Not a frown further**: no further by way of hostility.
33 **standing**: stagnant (cf. II. i. 216).   36 **demi-puppets**:
half-puppets (i.e. half the size of puppets)—fairies.   39 **mushrumps**: mushrooms.   43 **azur'd**: blue.   45 **rifted**: split. [*N*].

With his own bolt: the strong-bas'd promontory
Have I made shake; and by the spurs pluck'd up
The pine and cedar: graves at my command
Have wak'd their sleepers, op'd, and let them forth
By my so potent art. But this rough magic   50
I here abjure; and, when I have requir'd
Some heavenly music,—which even now I do,—
To work mine end upon their senses that
This airy charm is for, I'll break my staff,
Bury it certain fathoms in the earth,   55
And deeper than did ever plummet sound,
I'll drown my book.   [*Solemn music.*

> *Re-enter* ARIEL: *after him,* ALONSO, *with a frantic
> gesture, attended by* GONZALO; SEBASTIAN *and* ANTONIO
> *in like manner, attended by* ADRIAN *and* FRANCISCO:
> *they all enter the circle which* PROSPERO *had made, and
> there stand charmed; which* PROSPERO *observing, speaks.*

A solemn air and the best comforter
To an unsettled fancy, cure thy brains,
Now useless, boil'd within thy skull! There stand,   60
For you are spell-stopp'd.
Holy Gonzalo, honourable man,
Mine eyes, even sociable to the show of thine,
Fall fellowly drops. The charm dissolves apace;
And as the morning steals upon the night,   65
Melting the darkness, so their rising senses
Begin to chase the ignorant fumes that mantle

47 spurs: roots.   **49 op'd:** opened.   **51 requir'd:** re-
quested, called for.   **53-4 their senses . . . for:** the senses of
those for whose benefit, &c. [*N*].   **57 book:** i.e. of magic (cf. III. ii.
90–3).   **58 A solemn air . . . best:** solemn music which is the
best. [*N*].   **62 Holy:** good, excellent.   **63 sociable to . . . thine:**
companiable to (i.e. in sympathy with) the (tearful) appearance of
yours.   **64 Fall fellowly drops:** let fall drops in sympathy.
67 mantle: cover with scum. [*N*].

Their clearer reason.—O good Gonzalo!
My true preserver, and a loyal sir
To him thou follow'st, I will pay thy graces   70
Home, both in word and deed.—Most cruelly
Didst thou, Alonso, use me and my daughter:
Thy brother was a furtherer in the act;—
Thou'rt pinch'd for 't now, Sebastian.—Flesh and blood,
You, brother mine, that entertain'd ambition,   75
Expell'd remorse and nature; who, with Sebastian,—
Whose inward pinches therefore are most strong,—
Would here have kill'd your king; I do forgive thee,
Unnatural though thou art!—Their understanding
Begins to swell, and the approaching tide   80
Will shortly fill the reasonable shores
That now lie foul and muddy. Not one of them
That yet looks on me, or would know me.—Ariel,
Fetch me the hat and rapier in my cell:—   [*Exit* ARIEL.
I will discase me, and myself present,   85
As I was sometime Milan.—Quickly, spirit;
Thou shalt ere long be free.

ARIEL *re-enters, singing, and helps to attire* PROSPERO.

Ariel. Where the bee sucks, there suck I:
        In a cowslip's bell I lie;
        There I couch when owls do cry,   90
        On the bat's back I do fly
        After summer merrily:
        Merrily, merrily shall I live now
        Under the blossom that hangs on the bough.

Prospero. Why, that's my dainty Ariel! I shall miss thee;

---

69 **sir**: gentleman.   71 **Home**: thoroughly.   76 **remorse**:
pity.   **nature**: i.e. natural feeling.   81 **reasonable shores**:
shores of the reason.   85 **discase me**: undress myself (i.e. throw
off his magic robe, &c.).   86 **sometime Milan**: formerly Duke
of Milan.   90 **couch**: lie.   92 **After**: in pursuit of.

But yet thou shalt have freedom;—so, so, so.—   96
To the king's ship, invisible as thou art:
There shalt thou find the mariners asleep
Under the hatches; the master and the boatswain
Being awake, enforce them to this place,   100
And presently, I prithee.

   Ariel. I drink the air before me, and return
Or e'er your pulse twice beat.   *[Exit.*

   Gonzalo. All torment, trouble, wonder, and amaze-
ment
Inhabits here: some heavenly power guide us   105
Out of this fearful country!

   Prospero.   Behold, sir king,
The wronged Duke of Milan, Prospero.
For more assurance that a living prince
Does now speak to thee, I embrace thy body;
And to thee and thy company I bid   110
A hearty welcome.

   Alonso.   Whe'r thou beest he or no,
Or some enchanted trifle to abuse me,
As late I have been, I not know: thy pulse
Beats, as of flesh and blood; and, since I saw thee,
Th' affliction of my mind amends, with which,   115
I fear, a madness held me: this must crave,—
And if this be at all—a most strange story.
Thy dukedom I resign, and do entreat
Thou pardon me my wrongs.—But how should Prospero
Be living, and be here?

---

   99 Under the hatches: below deck.   **100 Being awake:**
when they are awake.   **enforce them:** compel them (to come).
[*N*].   **101 presently:** immediately.   **103 Or e'er:** before.
111 Whe'r: whether.   **112 enchanted trifle:** trick, deceptive
appearance, due to magic.   **abuse:** deceive.   **113 late:** lately.
have been: i.e. have been deceived.   **116 crave:** demand.
117 And if . . . at all: If this has any real existence, i.e. if I am not
just dreaming.   **119 my wrongs:** the wrongs I have done (cf. l. 25).

Prospero.   First, noble friend,   120
Let me embrace thine age; whose honour cannot
Be measur'd, or confin'd.

Gonzalo.   Whether this be,
Or be not, I'll not swear.

Prospero.   You do yet taste
Some subtilties o' the isle, that will not let you
Believe things certain.—Welcome! my friends all:—   125
[*Aside to* SEBASTIAN *and* ANTONIO.] But you, my brace of
          lords, were I so minded,
I here could pluck his highness' frown upon you,
And justify you traitors: at this time
I will tell no tales.

Sebastian. [*Aside.*] The devil speaks in him.

Prospero..   No.
For you, most wicked sir, whom to call brother   130
Would even infect my mouth, I do forgive
Thy rankest fault; all of them; and require
My dukedom of thee, which, perforce, I know,
Thou must restore.

Alonso.   If thou beest Prospero,
Give us particulars of thy preservation;   135
How thou hast met us here, who three hours since
Were wrack'd upon this shore; where I have lost,—
How sharp the point of this remembrance is!—
My dear son Ferdinand.

Prospero.   I am woe for 't, sir.

Alonso. Irreparable is the loss, and patience   140
Says it is past her cure.

Prospero.   I rather think

---

121 **thine age:** you who are an old man.   124 **subtilties:**
delicacies.   [*N*].   125 **things certain:** things that are certain.
128 **justify:** prove.   132 **all of them:** all thy faults.   **require:**
call for, demand (cf. l. 51).   139 **woe:** sorry.   140-1 **patience
. . . cure:** I cannot learn to bear it patiently.

You have not sought her help; of whose soft grace,
For the like loss I have her sovereign aid,
And rest myself content.
   Alonso.   You the like loss!
   Prospero. As great to me, as late; and, supportable   145
To make the dear loss, have I means much weaker
Than you may call to comfort you, for I
Have lost my daughter.
   Alonso.   A daughter?
O heavens! that they were living both in Naples,
The king and queen there! that they were, I wish   150
Myself were mudded in that oozy bed
Where my son lies. When did you lose your daughter?
   Prospero. In this last tempest. I perceive, these lords
At this encounter do so much admire
That they devour their reason, and scarce think   155
Their eyes do offices of truth, their words
Are natural breath: but, howsoe'r you have
Been justled from your senses, know for certain
That I am Prospero and that very duke
Which was thrust forth of Milan; who most strangely   160
Upon this shore, where you were wrack'd, was landed,
To be the lord on't. No more yet of this;
For 'tis a chronicle of day by day,
Not a relation for a breakfast nor
Befitting this first meeting. Welcome, sir;   165
This cell's my court: here have I few attendants

---

142 **of whose soft grace**: by whose gentle favour.   145 **late**:
recent.   145–6 **supportable . . . loss**: to make the bitter loss supportable. [*N*].   150 **that**: provided that. [*N*].   151 **mudded**:
embedded in mud (cf. III. iii. 102).   154 **admire**: wonder.
155 **devour their reason**: i.e. are open-mouthed with wonder.
156 **do offices of truth**: perform their functions truly, tell the
truth.   156–7 **their words . . . breath**: that they hear and
speak awake. [*N*].   158 **justled**: jostled, hustled.   160 **of**:
from.   162 **on't**: cf. I. ii. 87, &c.

And subjects none abroad: pray you, look in.
My dukedom since you have given me again,
I will requite you with as good a thing;
At least bring forth a wonder, to content ye   170
As much as me my dukedom.

> *The entrance of the Cell opens, and discovers* FERDI-
> NAND *and* MIRANDA *playing at chess.*

Miranda. Sweet lord, you play me false.
Ferdinand.   No, my dearest love,
I would not for the world.
Mira. Yes, for a score of kingdoms you should wrangle,
And I would call it fair play.
Alonso.   If this prove   175
A vision of the island, one dear son
Shall I twice lose.
Sebastian.   A most high miracle!
Ferdinand. Though the seas threaten, they are merciful:
I have curs'd them without cause.

> [*Kneels to* ALONSO.
Alonso.   Now, all the blessings
Of a glad father compass thee about!   180
Arise, and say how thou cam'st here.
Miranda.   O, wonder!
How many goodly creatures are there here!
How beauteous mankind is! O brave new world,
That has such people in 't!
Prospero.   'Tis new to thee.
Alonso. What is this maid, with whom thou wast at play?
Your eld'st acquaintance cannot be three hours: 186

---

167 **abroad:** i.e. outside the island (or the cell).   (*s.d.*) *dis-*
covers: reveals.   172 **play me false:** cheat (me).   174
score: twenty. [*N*].   183 **brave:** cf. I. ii. 6.   186 **eld'st:**
at the longest.

Is she the goddess that hath sever'd us,
And brought us thus together?
   Ferdinand.   Sir, she is mortal;
But by immortal Providence she's mine;
I chose her when I could not ask my father   190
For his advice, nor thought I had one. She
Is daughter to this famous Duke of Milan,
Of whom so often I have heard renown,
But never saw before; of whom I have
Receiv'd a second life; and second father   195
This lady makes him to me.
   Alonso.   I am hers:
But O! how oddly will it sound that I
Must ask my child forgiveness!
   Prospero.   There, sir, stop:
Let us not burden our remembrances
With a heaviness that's gone.
   Gonzalo.   I have inly wept,   200
Or should have spoke ere this. Look down, you gods,
And on this couple drop a blessed crown;
For it is you that have chalk'd forth the way
Which brought us hither!
   Alonso.   I say, Amen, Gonzalo!
   Gonzalo. Was Milan thrust from Milan, that his issue 205
Should become kings of Naples? O, rejoice
Beyond a common joy, and set it down
With gold on lasting pillars. In one voyage
Did Claribel her husband find at Tunis,
And Ferdinand, her brother, found a wife   210

   193 renown: report.   **194 But never:** i.e. but (whom I)
never.   **196 I am hers:** i.e. I am henceforward a second father
to her (as Prospero is to Ferdinand).   **199 remembrances:**
memories.   **200 heaviness:** sorrow.   **203 chalk'd forth:**
marked out.   **204 Amen:** so be it!   **205 Milan . . .**
Milan: the Duke . . . the city.

Where he himself was lost; Prospero his dukedom
In a poor isle; and all of us ourselves,
When no man was his own.

    Alonso. [*To* FERDINAND *and* MIRANDA.] Give me your
        hands:
Let grief and sorrow still embrace his heart
That doth not wish you joy!

    Gonzalo.   Be it so: Amen!   **215**

     Re-enter ARIEL, *with the* Master *and* Boatswain
     amazedly following.

O look, sir! look, sir! here are more of us.
I prophesied, if a gallows were on land,
This fellow could not drown.—Now, blasphemy,
That swear'st grace o'erboard, not an oath on shore?
Hast thou no mouth by land? What is the news?   **220**

    Boatswain. The best news is that we have safely found
Our king and company: the next, our ship,—
Which but three glasses since we gave out split,—
Is tight and yare and bravely rigg'd as when
We first put out to sea.

    Ariel. [*Aside to* PROSPERO.] Sir, all this service   **225**
Have I done since I went.

    Prospero. [*Aside to* ARIEL.] My tricksy spirit!

    Alonso. These are not natural events; they strengthen
From strange to stranger.—Say, how came you hither?

    Boatswain. If I did think, sir, I were well awake,
I'ld strive to tell you. We were dead of sleep,   **230**

    213 **his own**: in his right senses.   214 **still**: for ever.   217
if a gallows were: if there existed a gallows (see I. i. 29–31).   218
blasphemy: you blaspheming fellow.   219 **grace**: the grace
of God. [*N*].   223 **glasses**: cf. I. ii. 240. [*N*].   **gave out**:
reported.   224 **yare**: in good trim (cf. I. i. 6).   226
tricksy: full of tricks, resourceful.   227–8 **strengthen...stranger**:
increase more and more in strangeness.   230 **dead of sleep**: in
a profound sleep.

And,—how we know not,—all clapp'd under hatches,
Where, but even now, with strange and several noises
Of roaring, shrieking, howling, jingling chains,
And mo diversity of sounds, all horrible,
We were awak'd; straightway, at liberty: 235
Where we, in all her trim, freshly beheld
Our royal, good, and gallant ship; our master
Capering to eye her: on a trice, so please you,
Even in a dream, were we divided from them,
And were brought moping hither.

    Ariel. [*Aside to* PROSPERO.] Was't well done?   240

    Prospero. [*Aside to* ARIEL.] Bravely, my diligence! Thou
    shalt be free.

    Alonso. This is as strange a maze as e'er men trod;
And there is in this business more than nature
Was ever conduct of: some oracle
Must rectify our knowledge.

    Prospero.   Sir, my liege,   245
Do not infest your mind with beating on
The strangeness of this business: at pick'd leisure
Which shall be shortly, single I'll resolve you,—
Which to you shall seem probable,—of every
These happen'd accidents; till when, be cheerful,   250
And think of each thing well.—[*Aside to* ARIEL.] Come
    hither, spirit;

232 **strange and several**: different strange.   234 **mo**: more.
236 **Where**: on which occasion, when. [*N*].   238 **on a trice**: in a
trice, moment. [*N*].   239 **them**: i.e. the crew.   240 **moping**:
moving in bewilderment.   241 **Bravely, my diligence**: excel-
lently, my diligent (spirit).   244 **conduct of**: conductor of,
instrumental in bringing about (cf. l. 227).   246 **infest**: harass,
trouble. **beating on**: hammering at, reasoning about (cf. I. ii. 176;
IV. i. 163).   247 **pick'd**: chosen.   248 **single**: alone in
private. [*N*]. **resolve you**: free you from perplexity.   249
Which: which (resolution), i.e. explanation. [*N*].   249–50. **every
These happen'd accidents**: every one of those events that have
occurred.   251 **well**: as being for the best.

Set Caliban and his companions free;
Untie the spell. [*Exit* ARIEL.] How fares my gracious sir?
There are yet missing of your company
Some few odd lads that you remember not   255

> *Re-enter* ARIEL, *driving in* CALIBAN, STEPHANO, *and*
> TRINCULO, *in their stolen apparel.*

Stephano. Every man shift for all the rest, and let no man
take care for himself, for all is but fortune.—Coragio!
bully-monster, Coragio!

Trinculo. If these be true spies which I wear in my head,
here's a goodly sight.   260

Caliban. O Setebos! these be brave spirits, indeed.
How fine my master is! I am afraid
He will chastise me.

Sebastian.   Ha, ha!
What things are these, my lord Antonio?
Will money buy them?

Antonio.   Very like; one of them   265
Is a plain fish, and, no doubt, marketable.

Prospero. Mark but the badges of these men, my lords,
Then say if they be true.—This mis-shapen knave,—
His mother was a witch; and one so strong
That could control the moon, make flows and ebbs,   270
And deal in her command without her power.
These three have robb'd me; and this demi-devil,—
For he's a bastard one,—had plotted with them
To take my life: two of these fellows you
Must know and own; this thing of darkness I   275
Acknowledge mine.

255 **odd**: not included among the others.   257 **Coragio!**:
Courage!   258 **bully-monster**: gallant monster. [*N*].   259 **If
these ... head**: if I can trust the eyes in my head.   261 **Setebos!**:
cf. I. ii. 373. [*N*].   266 **a plain fish**: clearly a fish.   271 **deal
in her command ... power**: wield her (i.e. the moon's) authority
without actually having the moon's power.

Caliban.   I shall be pinch'd to death

Alonso. Is not this Stephano, my drunken butler?

Sebastian. He is drunk now: where had he wine?

Alonso. And Trinculo is reeling-ripe: where should they
Find this grand liquor that hath gilded them?   280
How cam'st thou in this pickle?

Trinculo. I have been in such a pickle since I saw you
last that, I fear me, will never out of my bones: I shall not
fear fly-blowing.

Sebastian. Why, how now, Stephano!   285

Stephano. O! touch me not: I am not Stephano, but a
    cramp.

Prospero. You'd be king of the isle, sirrah?

Stephano. I should have been a sore one then.

Alonso. This is a strange thing as e'er I look'd on.

                      [*Pointing to* CALIBAN.

Prospero. He is as disproportion'd in his manners   290
As in his shape.—Go, sirrah, to my cell;
Take with you your companions: as you look
To have my pardon, trim it handsomely.

Caliban. Ay, that I will; and I'll be wise hereafter,
And seek for grace. What a thrice-double ass   295
Was I, to take this drunkard for a god,
And worship this dull fool!

Prospero.   Go to; away!

Alonso. Hence, and bestow your luggage where you
    found it.

Sebastian. Or stole it, rather.

         [*Exeunt* CALIBAN, STEPHANO, *and* TRINCULO.

279 **reeling-ripe:** completely drunk. [*N*].   279–80 **where
should they Find:** where can they have found?   280 **gilded:**
given a flush to (their faces).   281 **pickle:** sorry plight.
283 **that:** as. [*N*].   288 **sore:** (1) aching, (2) severe.   289
a strange thing as e'er: as strange a thing as ever.   290
disproportion'd: ill-conditioned.   292 **as you look:** in so far
as you expect.   298 **luggage:** cf. IV. i. 230.

Prospero. Sir, I invite your highness and your train   300
To my poor cell, where you shall take your rest
For this one night; which—part of it—I'll waste
With such discourse as, I not doubt, shall make it
Go quick away; the story of my life
And the particular accidents gone by   305
Since I came to this isle: and in the morn
I'll bring you to your ship, and so to Naples,
Where I have hope to see the nuptial
Of these our dear-beloved solemniz'd;
And thence retire me to my Milan, where   310
Every third thought shall be my grave.
   Alonso.   I long
To hear the story of your life, which must
Take the ear strangely.
   Prospero.   I'll deliver all;
And promise you calm seas, auspicious gales
And sail so expeditious that shall catch   315
Your royal fleet far off.—[*Aside to* ARIEL.] My Ariel, chick,
That is thy charge: then to the elements
Be free, and fare thou well!—Please you, draw near.
                                                 [*Exeunt.*

EPILOGUE

Spoken by PROSPERO

Now my charms are all o'erthrown,
  And what strength I have's mine own;
Which is most faint: now, 'tis true,
  I must be here confin'd by you,
Or sent to Naples. Let me not,   5
  Since I have my dukedom got

---

305 **particular**: in detail.   **accidents**: incidents.   308
nuptial: marriage.   313 **Take**: captivate.   **deliver all**: tell
(you) everything.   315 **sail**: sailing, voyage.   **catch**: over-
take.   316 **far off**: which has a long start.

And pardon'd the deceiver, dwell
In this bare island by your spell;
But release me from my bands
With the help of your good hands.   10
Gentle breath of yours my sails
Must fill, or else my project fails,
Which was to please. Now I want
Spirits to enforce, art to enchant;
And my ending is despair,   15
Unless I be reliev'd by prayer,
Which pierces so that it assaults
Mercy itself and frees all faults.
As you from crimes would pardon'd be,
Let your indulgence set me free.   20

NOTES

Folio = First Folio of 1623.

O.E.D. = *Oxford English Dictionary.*

References to other plays are made to the one volume Oxford
Shakespeare.

Textual notes and a few other more advanced notes are enclosed
within brackets, thus [   ].

ACT I. Scene I

'If you are an artist and are setting out to tell the incredible, nothing
will serve you so well as to open with absolute realism' (Quiller-
Couch). *The Tempest* opens in a whirl of action. Mariners are
running to and fro; the boatswain is shouting; thunder rolls over-
head; anxious passengers are appearing on deck. Such a scene immediately arrests the attention of an audience, and arouses curiosity
as to the fate of the passengers and crew. Part of a dramatist's
problem is to get hold of his audience quickly, to overcome its preliminary restlessness. Had Shakespeare opened the play with the
long conversation between Prospero and Miranda, his audience would
have taken far longer to settle down, and, while still noisy and rest-
less, they might have failed to catch—especially in an open-air
theatre—information that is vital to an understanding of what
follows.

1. **Boatswain!** The boatswain was in charge of the ship's sails,
   rigging, boats, anchors, &c. When the master issued an order, the
   boatswain summoned the men with his whistle before repeating the
   order.

2. **master.** On an Elizabethan merchant vessel the master, or
   master-mariner, was the Captain. On a man-of-war he ranked next
   to a lieutenant, and was entrusted with the navigation of the ship.
   The King of Naples would presumably be sailing in a man-of-war.

3. **Good:** an exclamation used in Elizabethan times, more often in
   the form 'Good now', to denote entreaty or expostulation. Here
   the meaning is almost = 'I pray you'. Cf. I. i. 14 and 18.

   [Folio punctuates 'Good:' which suggests that the intrepid master is
   replying to the boatswain's 'What cheer?' with an assurance that all
   is well. But his very next words make such an interpretation most
   unlikely.]

7. Blow, till thou burst ...: addressed most probably to the wind itself, 'wind' here being = 'lungs'. Cf. *Pericles*, III. i. 44, where, in identical circumstances, a sailor cries, 'Blow, and split thyself'. But possibly the boatswain is humorously telling the absent master to blow his whistle till he bursts, provided the ship has sea-room, i.e. so long as there is room to manœuvre the vessel.

9. Play the men: most probably the equivalent in the plural of 'Play the man!' But Professor Dover Wilson interprets 'Pipe all hands'. There seems no point, however, in issuing such an order at this stage in the storm: the men had presumably been 'piped' on deck long before this.

13. assist the storm. Cf. *Pericles*, III. i. 19: 'do not assist the storm.' The whole of this scene should be compared with *Pericles*, III. i.

15. cares. Examples of a plural subject followed by a singular verb are common in Shakespeare, and occur fairly frequently in this play. But 'cares' here is simply the old Northern plural form of the verb, which was still quite commonly used in the early seventeenth century. (Cf. I. ii. 475, and see Appendix II, Verbs.)

15-16. these roarers: the waves. A 'roarer' was also a term for a wild, roistering fellow. Shakespeare may have visualized the waves as lurching and staggering.

20. counsellor. 'Gonzalo was a member of the King's Council, whose business it was to quell riots and "work the peace".' (Dover Wilson.)

28-9. his complexion ... gallows: 'he looks as if he were certainly destined for the gallows'. Gonzalo is referring to the proverb, 'He that is born to be hanged will never be drowned'. 'Complexion' is a word from medieval physiology, used to designate the combination in the human body of certain qualities or humours (hot, cold, moist, dry). The nearest equivalent to the word in its original sense would be 'temperament'.

36. our office. The boatswain was popularly represented as a noisy fellow, like the sergeant-major in modern times. He had, in any case, to make his shrill whistle heard above the gale.

46. Set her two courses. The sails attached to the lower yards of a ship (the 'fore-sail' and the 'main-sail') were known as 'courses' (the 'fore-course' and the 'main-course'). When the order to 'lay her a-hold' is given, one must suppose that the ship is lying into the wind with all her sails lowered. The boatswain, realizing that the only hope now is to try a new tack out to sea, calls on his men to hoist the sails again, on the chance that the vessel may clear the shore. But it is too late.

[Folio punctuates 'Set her two courses off to Sea again'. 'Courses' also meant 'points of the compass', and 'Set her two courses off to sea again' would be 'Shift her course two points of the compass out to sea again'.]

49. must our mouths be cold? The boatswain is probably thinking of the cold sea-water that he and his mates will soon be swallowing; but the phrase 'cold i' the mouth' occurs in Beaumont and Fletcher's *Scornful Lady*, II. ii, as a synonym for 'dead'.

[It has also been suggested that at this point the boatswain pulls out a bottle of rum from his pocket, and gulps down some of the fiery liquor. Others interpret the boatswain's remark as a reference to the prayers just mentioned, i.e. 'Must our mouths be cold with praying?']

53. wide-chapp'd. Antonio probably refers to the mouth of the boatswain, wide open from his constant bawling of orders, but he may be following up his remark about drunkards, and thinking of the boatswain with a bottle held to his mouth.

53–4. would thou might'st . . . tides. In Elizabethan days captured pirates were regularly fastened to the shore at low-water mark until three tides had washed over them. Antonio shows his wrath with the boatswain by raising the tides to ten. In Gilbert's *Mikado* the Mikado similarly thinks of 'something lingering' for his victim.

62. long heath, brown furze. Heath alone would mean 'barren country', and perhaps 'long heath' *might* mean a wide extent of this, but since early botanists call *Erica vulgaris* 'long' it seems more likely that Shakespeare makes Gonzalo despise his most miserable piece of dry land as that which will grow only heather. The picture has a different appeal to modern romantic taste for wild country.

[This passage has been much annotated. Among the emendations suggested is 'Ling (i.e. heather), heath, broom, furze'. Folio reads 'Long heath, Browne firrs', i.e. fir trees, which perhaps should be restored to the text, though 'sharp furzes' occurs in IV. i. 180.]

61–4. 'It may be observed of Gonzalo, that, being the only good man that appears with the King, he is the only man that preserves his cheerfulness in the wreck and his hope on the island.' (Johnson.)

ACT I. Scene II

The quiet and repose of this scene following upon the confusion of the first provide an immediate contrast. A considerable part of it is narrative, but narrative worked so naturally and dramatically into dialogue form, and so interesting in itself, that one never stops to reflect that almost nothing is happening in this scene at all. The magic, however, which pervades the play now appears for the first time in several small incidents.

1-13. Miranda's opening speech, besides telling a good deal about Miranda's character, would serve to indicate in a general way to an Elizabethan audience the locality of the second scene.

1. In addressing her father, Miranda always uses the respectful 'you' and 'your'. Prospero—a father speaking to a daughter—employs the familiar or tender 'thou' and 'thine'. This distinction, now lost in English, is still active in French.

3-5. **The sky . . . out.** The sky is black with storm-clouds—'pitch' black. From time to time a streak of lightning ('the fire') runs through the clouds; and, thinking of pitch boiling in a cauldron, with a fire flaring beneath it, Shakespeare imagines the pitch-black clouds melting in the sky and pouring forth their contents upon the earth below. But immediately he pictures the stormy sea, where the waves are rising so high that they seem to reach the lightning-riven clouds, and so 'dash the fire out'. For 'cheek', cf. *Richard II*, III. iii. 57, the 'cloudy cheeks of heaven'.—'Miranda is also thinking of "cheek" = the side of a grate.' (Dover Wilson.)

7. **some noble creatures.** 'The doubt here intimated could have occurred to no mind but to that of Miranda, who had been bred up in the island with her father and a monster only; she did not know, as others do, what sort of creatures were in a ship; others never would have introduced it as a conjecture.' (Coleridge.)

[Folio reads 'creature'. If that reading is retained, 'creature' must be a collective noun.]

14. **amazement.** In Elizabethan English the word can convey the idea of 'terror' and 'perplexity', as well as 'astonishment'. Cf. I. ii. 198.

15. **O, woe the day!** 'Miranda, when she speaks the words, "O, woe the day!" supposes, not that the crew had escaped, but that her father thought differently from her, and counted their destruction "no harm".' (Johnson.) Or, more naturally perhaps,

Miranda, like a grief-stricken child, does not respond immediately to the voice of comfort, being so full of the awful event she has just seen.

19. more better. 'More' was often prefixed to the comparative of adjective or adverb in Shakespeare's day. No extra emphasis need be implied. See Appendix II, p. 182.

22–3. 'Prospero's speeches, till the entrance of Ariel, contain the finest example I remember of retrospective narration for the purpose of putting the audience in possession of all the information necessary for the understanding of the plot. Observe, too, the perfect probability of the moment chosen by Prospero . . . to open out the truth to his daughter.' (Coleridge.)

28–31. The passage presents an apparent rather than a real difficulty. Prospero, intending to say that no one is in any danger, breaks off in the middle of his speech—'There is no soul (in danger)'—and makes a fresh start with 'No, not so much perdition', &c. This is a common enough fault in conversation, and Shakespeare is often colloquial in this way, owing, no doubt, to the rapidity with which he composed his plays. Cf. I. ii. 66–77.

> [Johnson, to avoid the sharp break in the construction, proposed to read 'soil', i.e. 'stain', 'spot'. Ariel remarks later in this scene (l. 218) that the garments of the shipwrecked party are unblemished.]

32. Which thou heard'st cry. The antecedent of 'which' may be (1) vessel, (2) any creature in the vessel.

43–4. Of anything . . . remembrance: 'tell me of any past impression that has remained in your memory'. The frequent inversions in Prospero's speeches are a feature of this play, and are characteristic of Shakespeare's later style in general.

50. backward and abysm. The adverb here is used as a noun. Shakespeare is visualizing the abstract conception of time that has passed. 'The vivid pictorial quality of Shakespeare's imagination causes him to be dissatisfied with all forms of expression which are colourless and abstract.' (Raleigh.)

66–77. Here again Prospero's syntax becomes involved. He never completes the sentence that he has begun, but makes a new departure with the words 'those being all my study', linking what follows to what went before by repeating the words 'my brother'. 'My brother, Antonio (who is your uncle)—please listen to what I am saying—(how terrible a thing it is) that a brother should be so treacherous!—(Antonio) the man whom, next to yourself, I loved best in the world, and whom I entrusted with the administration of my dukedom, which at that time was the chief (in Italy),

and I Prospero the first among dukes—(my dukedom, I say, was)
held to be the first in importance, and there was no other that even
approached it in the liberal arts—those (same liberal arts) being all
that I concerned myself with, I threw the administration over to
my brother, and ceased to maintain my position as a duke, being
carried away by, and wholly absorbed in, secret studies.'

70. **as at that time:** at that very time. The 'as' is not = 'because',
but emphasizes the 'that'.

78. **Dost thou attend me?** This is the first of several similar
remarks by Prospero. A long monologue is tiresome to both
audience and actors—the actor who has to speak it, and the other
actors who have to listen. Shakespeare accordingly breaks up
Prospero's lengthy narrative by making him appeal at intervals for
Miranda's attention. In this way Miranda can be brought into the
action naturally; the audience feel that they are listening to a conversation and not (as with a monologue) being directly addressed;
and there is a further dramatic advantage in the mere physical
contrast between two voices, the man's and the woman's.

81. **To trash for over-topping.** A hound that over-ran the rest of
the pack was checked ('trashed') by having a cord or rope fastened
to its neck.

83. **key.** Shakespeare began by thinking of a key inserted in a lock,
and then went on to think of the musical key used for tuning
instruments. Hence the 'tune' of l. 85.

93–6. i.e. 'just as a good man is often the father of a bad son, so my
faith in my brother's honesty produced in him a falseness, which,
in its opposite way, was as great as my belief in him'.

98. **revenue.** The accent is on the second syllable.

100–2. **Who having . . . lie.** The meaning is clear enough, viz.
'who, by often telling a lie, has come to believe it himself'; and the
tortured expression is thoroughly Shakespearian. If the text is to
stand, the word 'it' must be taken as referring to 'lie', and 'into'
as equivalent to 'unto'. By telling the same lie over and over
again, one makes one's memory a sinner against truth, i.e. one
forgets that the lie *is* a lie.

107–8. **To have no screen . . . it for.** Antonio wished that there
might be nothing separating the part he was playing from the
reality, i.e. he wished to be in reality, as he was in effect, the sole
governor of Milan. The metaphor appears to be drawn from the
stage, the screen being that which concealed the prompter from the
audience.

109. Me, poor man. One must either supply 'for' or 'as for' before 'me'; or else one must suppose that Prospero is once more breaking off abruptly in the middle of a sentence.

114. his coronet to his crown. The first 'his' refers to Antonio, the second to Alonso. A 'coronet' is worn by a duke, a crown, by a king.

132. thy crying self. 'The power of poetry is, by a single word perhaps, to instil that energy into the mind, which compels the imagination to produce the picture. Here, by introducing a single happy epithet, "crying", a complete picture is presented to the mind, and in the production of such pictures the power of genius consists.' (Coleridge.)

146. butt. Prospero does not, of course, mean this word to be taken literally. He is speaking only of the 'rotten tub' upon which he was put to sea.

[Many editors, unnecessarily, adopt Rowe's conjecture, 'boat'.]

151. Did us but loving wrong: a conceit. The sighs of the wind are fancifully taken to be sighs of pity, and the wind is therefore 'loving'. But the practical result of the wind's sighs is to raise a greater commotion in the waves, and in this sense the wind does Prospero and his daughter a wrong.

152. Cherubin is a Hebrew plural, but as late as the eighteenth century the form 'cherubin' was popularly used for the singular, and 'cherubins' for the plural.

155. deck'd. There seems little reason for Prospero's saying that he 'decked' (i.e. 'adorned') the sea with his tears; but this was apparently Shakespeare's intention in using the word. He was probably thinking of Prospero's tear-drops adorning the ocean as 'drops' (i.e. small ornaments of glass or precious stone) often adorned an Elizabethan garment. Such an idea is highly artificial, no doubt, but Shakespeare occasionally startles one with just such an extravagant conceit. Cf. 'The fringed curtains of thine eye advance' (I. ii. 405).

[Some editors explain 'deck'd' as 'sprinkled'. Others take refuge in emendation, e.g. 'mock'd', 'fleck'd', 'dew'd', 'eked' (i.e. 'added to the saltness of'.]

162. who being. This is probably the result of hasty writing, and not an example of Elizabethan English. Two different constructions have been ungrammatically combined, viz. 'being then appointed', and 'who was then appointed'.

168–9. Would I might . . . man: an instance of 'dramatic irony'. The audience knows that Gonzalo is very much nearer to Miranda at this moment than she imagines.

169. Now I arise. Prospero rises to put on his magic cloak again, because Miranda's words about Gonzalo have brought him back to the immediate present. He is about to exert his spells to bring Gonzalo and the others to his cell.

173. princes: 'princes' must include 'princesses'. Prospero is saying: 'The children of most kings and dukes spend time in frivolities and have less careful tutors than I am to you.'

> [Folio has 'Princesse', which is probably a compositor's error. Some editors retain the Folio reading, but add an apostrophe ('princess'') to denote the plural, i.e. 'princesses').

181. zenith. Prospero speaks as an astrologer. In the seventeenth century the influence of the stars on men's fortunes was still widely credited. The thought of this passage is almost identical with that in *Julius Caesar* (IV. iii. 217–20):

> 'There is a tide in the affairs of men,
> Which, taken at the flood, leads on to fortune;
> Omitted, all the voyage of their life
> Is bound in shallows and in miseries.'

186. I know thou canst not choose: presumably another result of Prospero's 'art'.

188. Approach, my Ariel . . . Coleridge points out that Ariel and Miranda never meet, and suggests as the reason that 'the natural and human of the one and the supernatural of the other' would tend to neutralize each other.

198. I flam'd amazement. A fine imaginative phrase to describe the effect of Ariel appearing like lightning. Cf. the account in William Strachey's *A True Repertory*, Appendix IV, p. 189.

201. Jove's lightnings: cf. v. i. 45 and note.

212. [Then all a-fire with me. Folio punctuates here:—

> '. . . quit the vessell;
> Then all a fire with me the Kings sonne Ferdinand. . . .'

If this is what Shakespeare wrote, then Ariel is saying that he so flamed about Ferdinand that the King's son—not the ship—was 'all afire' with him.]

218. sustaining. This word is generally taken to indicate that the garments of the shipwrecked passengers bore them up in the water;

but perhaps not even Elizabethan clothes were likely to do that. 'Sustaining', therefore, may mean 'withstanding', i.e. 'withstanding the salt water', or perhaps simply 'undergoing immersion'.

[Shakespeare, who wrote at a great pace, may have thought first of the clothes being unstained, and then, as he proceeded to express this idea with the words 'not a blemish', the word 'stain' (which he had not yet used) may have lingered in his mind, and suggested 'sustaining'.]

224. in this sad knot. Ariel demonstrates what he means. To sit or stand with folded arms was, to the Elizabethans, a sure sign of melancholy. Cf. Biron in *Love's Labour's Lost* (III. i. 191–2) who describes Cupid as 'lord of folded arms, the anointed sovereign of sighs and groans'.

229. Bermoothes. The Bermudas were notorious among Elizabethan seamen for their violent storms.

234. flote. The meaning of 'flote' is doubtful, though it is generally explained as 'sea'. 'Flote', however, certainly means, in some contexts, 'flotilla' or 'fleet', and 'upon the Mediterranean flote' may = 'making for the Mediterranean flotilla'. (Dover Wilson.)

240. At least two glasses. Why does Prospero ask the time of day if he knows it? The words are given by some editors to Ariel; but 'it is common to ask a question which the next moment enables us to answer'. (Johnson.) Shakespeare in this play thinks of a glass as an hour-glass (cf. v. i. 186 and 223), though the Elizabethan seaman's glass was a half-hour glass. The time is therefore a little after two o'clock. The whole action of the play takes place in three to four hours.

250. To bate me a full year. It has been pointed out that Ariel here is using the language of a London apprentice, suggesting that so many years' service had been agreed upon. Ariel is 'moody' (l. 244) because he is a spirit, and spirits by their very nature were supposed to be impatient of restraint.

261. O! was she so? Shakespeare suggests Prospero's indignation with great skill.—'Dost thou forget?'—'No.'—'Thou dost.'—'I do not, sir.'—'Thou liest.'—'Hast thou forgot her?'—'No, sir.'—'Thou hast.' The modern equivalent of 'O! was she so?' would be 'Oh, she was, was she?' Incidentally, some necessary information is imparted to the audience in a very natural fashion.

266. one thing she did. Shakespeare gives no clue as to what benefit Sycorax had conferred on Algiers. It was suggested by Charles Lamb that he may have had in mind the story of a witch who prevented Algiers from falling into the hands of Charles V in 1541 by raising a storm which scattered his fleet. Alternatively, the absence of any explanation of what Sycorax did for Algiers may indicate a cut in the text if the play was ever revised.

269. blue-ey'd = haggard. Prospero is probably thinking not of the colour of the eyes themselves, but of the eyelids, or perhaps of the blue-black circles round the eyes caused by weeping, watching, &c.

281. strike. Shakespeare is no doubt thinking of the water from a mill-stream pouring out of one section of the mill-wheel into another as it revolves. Cf. the following definition of the word given by a writer in 1725: 'A very large fire engine for draining the coal pits . . . strikes (as they term it) or makes a discharge fourteen times in one minute.' (*O.E.D.*)

298. after two days. Ariel's service ends with the sailing of the ship on the following day. Cf. v. i. 316–18.

301. a nymph of the sea. Why should Ariel transform himself into a nymph if only Prospero is to see him? The answer can only be that this is an eminently spectacular play, and the change is made for theatrical rather than dramatic reasons, i.e. for the pleasure of the *audience*.

314. There's wood enough within. 'Another instance of admirable judgement and excellent preparation is to be found in the creature contrasted with Ariel,—Caliban; who is described in such a manner by Prospero as to lead us to expect the appearance of a foul, unnatural monster. He is not seen at once; his voice is heard; this is the preparation; he was too offensive to be seen at first in all his deformity, and in nature we do not receive so much disgust from sound as from sight.' (Coleridge.)

321–2. wicked dew . . . with raven's feather. Did Sycorax, the witch, transform herself into a raven and fly by night? The ordinary witch flew on a broomstick, but Sycorax was no ordinary one.—'It is said that raven's birds be fed with dew of heaven all the time that they have no black feathers by benefit of age.' (*Batman upon Bartholome*, 1582.) The commentators have done little to elucidate this curse of Caliban's.

323. south-west. Shakespeare frequently refers to the unwholesome effects of the south or south-west wind. Cf. *Cymbeline*, II. iii. 136: 'The south-fog rot him!'

326. urchins. Prospero may mean only that his power, exerted over the animal kingdom, will make the urchins (hedgehogs) annoy Caliban. But 'urchin' in Shakespeare's day also meant 'goblin', 'elf', and that may be the sense intended here.

327. vast of night: cf. 'the dead waste and middle of the night'. *Hamlet*, I. ii. 198.

328–30. thou shalt . . . 'em: i.e. you shall have as many pinches as there are cells in a honeycomb, and each pinch will sting you worse than the sting of bees that make those cells.

334. water with berries in 't. See Appendix IV for Strachey's mention of those berries.

335. the bigger light . . . the less. Shakespeare very skilfully suggests the savagery of Caliban by these vague references to sun and moon. See p. 173 for a criticism of Caliban's language.

351. Abhorred slave . . .

[In the Folio this speech is given to Miranda, but most editors prefer to assign it to Prospero. The tone of the speech is certainly more in keeping with Prospero's normal utterance than with his daughter's.]

358. race: nature (literally 'species', and so the hereditary nature of that species).

364. red plague. To the Elizabethan doctor there were three forms of plague: the red, the yellow, the black (cf. 'Black Death'). What precisely the red plague was is a matter of dispute; but Shakespeare probably used 'red' here because the sound of the word goes with 'rid', and so makes Caliban's curse more emphatic. Caliban's only regret at having learnt to speak is that when he uses this gift to curse Prospero he is punished for it.

369. old cramps: cramps which attack the aged. But 'old' has sometimes an intensive force, and is equivalent to 'great' or 'plentiful'. Cf. *Much Ado about Nothing*, v. ii. 102, 'Yonder's old coil at home'. 'Old cramps' may therefore = many (or great) cramps.

370. aches: pronounced 'aitches'.

373. dam's. This word subtly emphasizes the sub-human nature of Caliban. 'Dam' = 'mother' was not used of human beings except contemptuously; the term was normally restricted to animals. It appears also in the phrase 'the devil and his dam', where 'dam' is simply 'woman'—the devil's 'woman' being, of course, as Sycorax was, a witch.

Setebos: the supreme god of the Patagonians. He is mentioned in Eden's *History of Travel* (1577). Browning's *Caliban upon Setebos* takes its origin from this line. See Appendix V, p. 190.

(*s.d.*) ARIEL *invisible*. On the Elizabethan stage invisibility presented no difficulties. The actor wore a special 'robe to go invisible', and the audience accepted it as a normal stage convention.

377. kiss'd. A preliminary kiss, as well as a curtsy, was formerly a ceremonial feature of certain dances.

['Whist' is either an adjective, 'hushed', 'making no sound', or the past participle of the verb meaning 'to become or be silent'. Some editors, following the punctuation of the Folio, which has no stop at all after 'kiss'd', suppose that Ariel is inviting the sprites to 'kiss the wild waves into silence', but most take the fourth line of the song as a parenthesis, viz. 'the wild waves being hushed'.]

380. [The text accepts Theobald's emendation of the Folio, which reads: 'and sweete Sprightes beare the burthen.']

394. fathom. A fathom is the length measured by a man's out-stretched arms, from the finger-tips of one hand to those of the other: six feet.

395. are. Unless Shakespeare is using 'coral' as a collective noun followed by a plural verb, 'are' must be due to the attraction of the plural 'bones' immediately preceding it.

405. The fringed curtains . . .: i.e. lift up your eyelids, open your eyes. The eyelids are spoken of metaphorically as curtains; and the eye-lashes as the fringes. This line has been criticized on the score of artificiality. It is certainly an elaborate way of saying 'Look up'; but, as Coleridge has pointed out, the occasion is an important one. 'At this moment Prospero sees Ferdinand, and wishes to point him out to his daughter, not only with great, but with scenic solemnity, he standing before her, and before the spectator, in the dignified character of a great magician.'

[Cf. *Pericles*, III. ii. 99: 'Her eyelids . . . begin to part their fringes of bright gold.']

408. but: because spirits are usually incorporeal, but Ferdinand has a 'brave form'.

412. canker: 'a caterpillar, or any insect larva, which destroys the buds and leaves of plants' (*O.E.D.*). Cf. Milton, *Lycidas*: 'As kill-ing as the canker to the rose.'

418. the goddess. Note the symmetrical situation: Miranda takes Ferdinand for a spirit, Ferdinand takes Miranda for a goddess.

426. I am the best . . . speech. Ferdinand, convinced that his father is drowned, naturally assumes that he is now the King of Naples himself, and therefore 'the best' in Naples, where all others would be subject to him.

429. single. The word has various meanings, and Shakespeare is probably playing on them; viz. (1) solitary; (2) slight, feeble; (3) unmarried; (4) honest, free from deceit; (5) one and the same (i.e. himself and King of Naples).

435. his brave son. There is no other mention of Antonio's son in in the play. He may have been one of the *dramatis personae* in an earlier version of *The Tempest*. See the Introduction, p. 14.

436. more braver: cf. I. ii. 19.

460. fresh-brook mussels. The freshwater variety was hardly considered fit for human food. 'The River muskles are not for meate.' (*The Description of Pembrokeshire*, 1603—quoted in *O.E.D.*)

475. there is: cf. I. i. 15.

485. nor: another instance of rapid writing. Shakespeare appears to have intended Ferdinand to say '(Neither) my father's loss, nor . . . this man's threats have any power to move me', and then, when he expressed Ferdinand's indifference positively—'are but light to me'—he omitted to change the 'nor' to an 'or'.

[Many editors, however, assume the error to be a compositor's, and change to 'or'.]

ACT II. Scene I

The stage now fills again, and we listen to ten minutes of not very impressive Elizabethan wit, with the disconsolate Alonso silent in the midst of the foolish chatter and hearing none of it. The magic world returns with Ariel's 'solemn music'. Then comes an effective contrast: Antonio and Sebastian drop their banter and suddenly become serious. The revelation that Alonso and Gonzalo are in grave danger raises the dramatic tension considerably.

(*s.d.*) *and others.* Alonso is apparently attended by a number of gentlemen in addition to Sebastian, Antonio, Gonzalo, Adrian, and Francisco. In v. i. 300 Prospero invites Alonso and his 'train' to rest in his cell. The Elizabethans were accustomed to a full stage, and with so many scenes in which only two or three characters are present Alonso and his train of followers would provide a welcome contrast.

11. **visitor.** 'Gonzalo gives . . . comfort, and is therefore properly called "the visitor", like others who visit the sick or distressed to give them consolation.' (Johnson.) Cf. Matthew xxv. 36: 'I was sick, and ye visited me.'

13. **it will strike.** Striking or 'repeating' watches were invented about the beginning of the sixteenth century.

15. **One:** i.e. 'he has struck one'.

18. **dollar:** the English name for the German coin, thaler. Sebastian is punning on the word 'entertainer'. Gonzalo has just used it of one who entertains (i.e. harbours) grief: Sebastian is thinking (1) of the host of an inn who entertains guests, and (2) of the actor or other performer who entertains by his performance.

28. **Which, of he . . .:** an Elizabethan construction, not confined to Shakespeare. The 'of' seems to be almost equivalent to 'whether'.

40. **He could not miss it.** Sebastian has guessed that a 'yet' will be the next word to come from the lips of Adrian. It duly comes, and Antonio uses these words, i.e. 'it was bound to come'.

43. **Temperance.** Antonio is punning here on 'Temperance' used as a girl's name, chiefly among Puritan families. It is suggested by Professor Dover Wilson that he may be referring to the far from delicate Temperance who is a character in Chapman's *May Day*, published in 1611.

57. **mistake.** Sebastian is probably punning on 'misses' of the previous line.

62. **[glosses.** The singular 'gloss' would be more normal here. Perhaps Shakespeare wrote 'freshness and gloss, as being . . .' (Dover Wilson).]

64. **If but one of his pockets . . .** The point here, and in Sebastian's reply, is obscure. Antonio seems to be suggesting that Gonzalo's pockets were full of mud from his drenching in the sea.

66. **report.** Here Sebastian seems to be making a punning reference to Gonzalo's work as a counsellor to the King.

74. **widow Dido's time.** Dido was a daughter of the King of Tyre. She became a widow when her husband, Sichaeus, was murdered. Dido herself fled from Tyre with a number of ships, and founded the city of Carthage on the North African coast. According to Virgil, her death was caused by the refusal of Aeneas, who had been wrecked near Carthage, and with whom she had fallen in love, to marry her. On his sudden departure, she killed herself.

75. **Widow!** Antonio protests at the mention of the word 'widow'. Perhaps he is thinking of his own wife, who is now, in effect, a widow.

81. This Tunis, sir . . . The town of Tunis had grown up about ten miles south-west of where Carthage once stood.

84–5. the miraculous harp . . . houses too: Amphion's lyre. He was said by his music to have moved stones, and so to have built the walls of Thebes. Similarly Apollo was said to have raised the walls of Troy.

91. [Ay? Folio gives this exclamation to Gonzalo, and prints it without the mark of interrogation. But it seems naturally to belong to Alonso, who is just waking out of his sad reverie. Antonio's 'Why, in good time' will then refer to the King's reawakening.]

99. doublet: a close-fitting body garment, with or without sleeves, worn by men.

101. That sort was well fish'd for. Antonio may be thinking of Gonzalo's doublet in the sea among the fishes; but even Antonio usually manages to make his jokes a little clearer than that. The surface meaning is 'That qualification of yours, "in a sort" (i.e. "after a fashion"), took you a long time to catch'. (Gonzalo had hitherto maintained that his garments were every bit as clean as they had been before the wreck.)

110. [FRANCISCO. Sir, he may live. Folio gives these words to Francisco, but some editors would transfer them to Gonzalo. In a later passage of this scene (ll. 227–33) Antonio alludes to the attempt made by one of the lords to persuade Alonso that his son yet lives. The lord in question is certainly Gonzalo, and this seems to be the only speech in the play to which Antonio's words could refer. Francisco, at any rate, speaks only once again—his three words in III. iii. 40.]

117. o'er his wave-worn basis bow'd . . . The cliffs have been worn away by waves at their base, and overhang the beach.

122. [loose. Most editors emend to 'lose', but the Folio 'loose' (i.e. 'turn loose') conveys greater contempt by its metaphor of animal mating.]

124. Who hath cause . . . on't. The antecedent of 'who' may be 'she' (i.e. Claribel), or more probably, 'your eye'—in which case 'who' is used where we should now employ 'which'.

127–8. at Which end o' the beam . . . bow. The beam is the transverse bar from either end of which the scales of a balance are hung. 'Weigh'd' may be (1) 'was balanced (in her mind)', or (2) 'consider'd', 'pondered'. The verb 'should bow' has no subject; and Shakespeare may have mixed up two different constructions, viz. (1) 'She was undecided at which end the beam should bow', (2) 'She was undecided which end of the beam should bow'. In either case the meaning is not in doubt. 'She wavered between disinclination (for the husband) and obedience (to her father), and it was doubtful which way the scales would tip.'

131. **Than we bring men,** &c. Sebastian appears to be thinking of the widows in Naples in two senses: (1) those who are widows *now*, but will no longer be so if he and the other survivors can return, (2) those who will always be widows, because (as he believes) their husbands have perished in the storm.

132. **dearest.** The etymology of this word is uncertain, but it was probably derived from a different root from 'dear' = beloved, precious. 'Dear' = hard, severe, is frequently used by Shakespeare. Cf. *Richard II*, I. iii. 151: 'The dateless limit of thy dear exile.'

139. **Foul weather?** Some joke seems to be intended here, or else Sebastian's question is pointless. Is it possible that he pronounces 'weather' like 'water', and so puns on Gonzalo's last remark? 'Cloudy' (i.e. 'dirty') would suggest the link between weather and water. In that case Antonio's 'very foul' would be his comment on Sebastian's poor pun, and would itself extend the pun a little further.

140. **plantation.** Gonzalo is speaking of plantation in the sense of 'planting' a colony. In the seventeenth and eighteenth centuries the American colonies were known as 'the plantations', and we still speak of a 'planter'. Antonio and Sebastian, however, take the word in the sense of putting plants or seeds into the ground.

145. **no kind of traffic ...** Gonzalo's commonwealth is based on a passage in Montaigne's essay *Of the Cannibals*, which Shakespeare read in John Florio's translation (1603). 'It is a nation ... that hath no kinde of traffike, no knowledge of Letters, no intelligence of numbers, no name of magistrate, nor of politike superioritie; no contracts, no successions, no partitions, no occupation but idle; no respect of kindred, but common, no apparell but naturall, no manuring of lands, no use of wine, corne, or mettle. The very words that import lying, falshood, treason, dissimulations, covetousnes, envie, detraction, and pardon, were never heard of amongst them.'

163. **all idle.** Antonio is quoting Gonzalo's own words against himself (cf. l. 151), and punning on the word 'idle', which has the meaning of 'worthless', as in 'an idle fellow'.

165. **the golden age.** 'The first and best age of the world, in which, according to the Greek and Roman poets, mankind lived in a state of ideal prosperity and happiness, free from all trouble and crime.' (*O.E.D.*) It was followed by a silver age, and an age of lead.

'Save his majesty. By a statute of James I designed to prevent profanity in the theatres the name of 'God' might not be mentioned on the stage.

173–4. nothing to you: i.e. worthless compared to you. Gonzalo is, of course, punning on his previous use of 'nothing'.

178. sphere. To the ancient astronomers the universe consisted of a number of 'spheres', which were thought of as hollow shells, one outside another, all revolving round a fixed Earth in the centre, and containing severally the heavenly bodies. Thus there was one sphere for the sun, others for the moon, and the planets, and one for the fixed stars.

180. bat-fowling. The method was to take a lantern and frighten the birds out of the trees and bushes. They were then captured in nets, or knocked down with sticks. Sebastian would use the moon as his lantern. (Cf. Lyly's *Gallathea*, III. iii: 'When I list I can set a trap for the sun, catch the moon with lime-twigs, and go a bat-fowling for stars.')

[But Sebastian's words have a secondary meaning. 'Bat-fowling' was also a term used in the slang of the underworld for victimizing or 'gulling' the simple-minded. It is presumably this secondary meaning that accounts for Gonzalo's anger, which Antonio refers to in the next line.]

185. Go sleep, and hear us: a puzzling remark. Antonio appears to be suggesting that old Gonzalo will be such a comical sight when he is asleep that *then* they will laugh. Or perhaps 'Go sleep' means 'prepare to sleep', and 'hear us' indicates that Antonio and Sebastian will do all the laughing Gonzalo has asked for.

204. art thou waking? i.e. aren't you dreaming? Sebastian wants to make Antonio more explicit in his statements.

212. Thou dost snore distinctly. Sebastian is reverting to his own suggestion that Antonio is talking in his sleep. Here he seems to be saying: 'You may be asleep, but there is a lot of sense in your snores—you snore intelligibly.'

216. Trebles. Sebastian would be thrice the man that he is now. Why thrice? Perhaps Antonio means that with Ferdinand dead (as he believes him to be) Sebastian is already twice the man he was, i.e. he is heir to the throne of Naples. But if he kills Alonso he will be three times greater than he was originally, i.e. he will be King. It is hardly necessary, however, to take the meaning so literally. Shakespeare seems to be using 'trebles' here as equivalent to 'greatly increases'. Cf. *Merchant of Venice*, III. ii. 153: 'I would be trebled twenty times myself.'

[Some editors reject 'trebles' and read 'troubles': i.e. it is a trouble to Sebastian to concentrate on what Antonio is saying. But the change is quite unnecessary.]

Well; I am standing water: 'My fortunes are not advancing, it is true'; or, perhaps, 'I am open to suggestion' (because he is not at present moving in any direction).

221–2. **Ebbing men ... run:** i.e. People who go backward, not forward, in fortune usually owe it to their own fault. Cf. *Julius Caesar*, I. ii. 139–40:

> The fault, dear Brutus, is not in our stars,
> But in ourselves, that we are underlings.

Shakespeare seems to have in mind here a stream at its estuary. When the tide is in, the basin is full; when it is at ebb, the stream is shallow and insignificant.

226. **Thus, sir. . . .** After feeling his way carefully Antonio is now coming to his murderous suggestion. He still proceeds, however, by dark hints. The whole of this passage is highly dramatic, and an effective contrast to the flippant chatter in the earlier part of the scene. We watch some one being persuaded; we see the light gradually dawning in his mind, and all the time Alonso and Gonzalo are sleeping in front of our eyes in the most deadly peril.

227. **this lord:** i.e. Gonzalo. But see note to l. 110.

230. **he 's a spirit of persuasion.** Gonzalo, we must suppose, had been trying to persuade the King, without really believing it himself, that Ferdinand might be still alive. A spirit is only the shade of a real person, not flesh and blood; and so with Gonzalo's persuading—it was not real, but only a form assumed for the occasion.

231. **Professes.** Gonzalo is a counsellor: it is his profession to advise and persuade.

238. **But doubts discovery there.** Ambition has reached its utmost limits; all beyond is obscure and doubtful.

[The Folio reading is 'doubt', and many editors retain it. If 'doubt' is the true reading then either (1) it must depend upon 'cannot' in the previous line, i.e. 'cannot . . . but doubt', or (2) 'but doubt' may be equivalent to 'without doubting'.]

243. **post.** Apollo, the sun-god, gallops his steeds round the earth in a single day.

245. [**she that from whom ...** The printer is generally blamed here for corrupting the text. After printing three 'she that's' he may have set up a fourth in mistake for 'she' only. The meaning, however, is clear, viz. 'she, in coming from whom we were all engulfed by the sea'.]

246. cast. This word almost certainly suggested the 'act' and 'prologue' of the lines that follow. ('Cast' = to assign parts to the actors in a play.) This sense of 'cast' may govern 'to perform', in which case a comma should be put after 'destiny'.

255–61. Say, this were death ... chat. 'The scene of the intended assassination of Alonso and Gonzalo is an exact counterpart of the scene between Macbeth and his lady, only pitched in a lower key throughout, . . . and exhibiting the same profound management in the manner of familiarizing a mind, not immediately recipient, to the suggestion of guilt, by associating the proposed crime with something ludicrous or out of place,—something not habitually matter of reverence.' (Coleridge.)

264–5. And how does your content ... fortune? At least a dozen plausible explanations of this difficult passage might be given. Both 'content' and 'tender' have a wide variety of meanings in Elizabethan English: 'tender' = 'make tender', 'feel or act tenderly to', 'hold dear', 'regard', 'value'. Perhaps Antonio's question is dependent on the verb 'understand' of his previous speech, i.e. 'And do you understand how your happiness makes offer to you of good fortune?'

270. But, for your conscience,— 'Yes,' Sebastian interrupts, 'but what about your conscience?'

273–5. twenty consciences . . . molest! The interpretation of this passage depends on whether 'candied' is taken as 'coated with sugar', or as 'frozen'. Taking it in the first sense (like 'the candied tongue' in *Hamlet*, III. ii. 65) the meaning would seem to be: 'If there were twenty consciences standing between the dukedom and me, let them be sugared over, and let that sugar melt sooner than that they should trouble me.' In the second sense: 'If there were twenty consciences standing between the dukedom and me, let them be frozen or let them melt away sooner than trouble me.' (The 'or' may be justified on the grounds that Antonio is quite indifferent about what happens to his conscience, so long as it does not trouble him.)

281. This ancient morsel: i.e. Gonzalo. The actor for whom the part was originally written was apparently a little man ; or perhaps Antonio is referring contemptuously to Gonzalo's body shrunk with age.

294. [thee. Folio reads 'them', which may be correct ; but the only persons in danger of their lives are the King and Gonzalo, and so 'them' can hardly refer to the King and his followers. It is possible, of course,

that after addressing the sleeping Gonzalo Ariel makes his next remark direct to the audience, in which case 'them' would refer to the
King and Gonzalo. Some editors read 'friends' and some, 'these, his
friends'.]

303–4. [Why, how now ... looking? It has been suggested that these words
must have been spoken not by Alonso, but by Gonzalo, when he
wakens and sees Sebastian and Antonio. 'Ho, awake!' was presumably his warning cry to the King. This alteration would also agree
with Gonzalo's account of what happened (l. 313): 'I heard a humming ... I shak'd you, sir, and cry'd.']

307–11. Like bulls ... lions. The speeches of Sebastian and Antonio
are marked by the clumsy exaggeration of men forced to improvise
in a hurry.

ACT II. Scene II

So far we have had only a glimpse of Caliban, just enough to whet
our curiosity. We now get a more extended view of him, and begin
to realize his ignorant and savage nature more clearly when we see
him ready to worship the drunken butler. The broad comedy of this
scene is an effective contrast to the serious events which have just
occurred.

8–14. For every trifle ... madness. Prospero is not one of Shakespeare's best-loved characters, and his unattractiveness to many
readers may be partly explained by such passages as this. No
doubt Caliban deserves punishment, but there is something petty
and even cruel in Prospero's way of tormenting him. Cruelty to
Caliban is almost cruelty to an animal.

28. this fish painted. Trinculo is probably thinking of having a
representation of Caliban painted on a sign-board and set up outside a booth to attract holiday crowds.

32–3. a dead Indian. Attempts have been made to identify the dead
Indian; but there are too many candidates to make the attempt
worth while. Fleet Street was a favourite thoroughfare all the year
round for the exhibition of prodigies, 'savages and men of Ind',
and even mummified bodies. They were also on view at such
festivals as Bartholomew Fair, and similar spectacles are still to be
seen to-day at Blackpool in the holiday season.

40. the dregs of the storm: i.e. the last drops of the storm.
'Dregs' carries on the idea of the 'foul bombard' above.

s.d. STEPHANO: pronounced Stéphano (cf. v. i. 277). In *The Merchant
of Venice*, on the other hand, the metre requires Stepháno.

43. at a man's funeral. Stephano is probably thinking of himself as, to all intents and purposes, dead. He has been cast ashore on a desert island, and he believes that he is the sole survivor, and not likely to survive for long.

57-8. Do you put tricks upon 's . . . Ind? Stephano's question suggests that in Elizabethan days some of the savages exhibited in London were bogus. To the Elizabethan, 'Ind' might mean either America, where the Red Indians came from, or Asia. Most of the Indians to be seen in Shakespeare's London were probably American. The 'you' of Stephano's question seems to be indefinite. He is simply saying: 'Am I to have tricks played upon me . . .?'

59. your four legs. Stephano catches sight of Caliban's two legs and Trinculo's two legs projecting from under Caliban's gaberdine.

59-60. As proper a man . . . legs. Cf. *Julius Caesar*, I. i. 29: 'As proper men as ever trod upon neat's leather.' 'As proper a man as ever went on two legs' is a proverbial expression. Stephano humorously changes the 'two' to 'four' to adapt the expression to the apparent monster in front of him.

65. an ague. Caliban is shaking with fear.

70. Do not torment me, &c. Though this and several other speeches of Caliban's are printed as prose, nearly every utterance of Caliban is in verse (e.g. ll. 113-15), or (as here) in rhythmical prose. He is conceived poetically, in contrast to the comically prosaic Stephano and Trinculo.

79. thy trembling. Stephano's hands are shaking because he is drunk; but Caliban is alluding to the notion that trembling was one of the signs of being possessed by an evil spirit. (Cf. 'now Prosper works upon thee'.)

81-2. here is that . . . cat: an allusion to the proverb, 'Good liquor will make a cat speak.'

89. His forward voice . . . The 'forward voice' is Caliban's, the 'backward' one, Trinculo's. Shakespeare may have intended a play upon the word 'backward', which also meant 'unfavourable', e.g. in the phrase, 'a backward answer'.

92. Amen! The significance of this 'Amen!' is not clear, but probably Stephano, who has been pouring wine into Caliban's mouth, means to say, 'Stop! that's enough for that mouth.'

96-7. I have no long spoon: an allusion to the proverb, 'He that would sup with the devil must have a long spoon.' Some at least of Shakespeare's audience could probably remember seeing the Vice in some old morality play: he was often represented as supping with a long spoon from the same bowl as the devil.

119. which I made of the bark of a tree. Shakespeare feels the need of explaining how Stephano came to have a bottle on a desert island, but Stephano's explanation must not be examined too closely. In the theatre one would never think of wondering how Stephano managed to make his bottle: one might wonder where he got the bottle from. He has told us, and that is enough. A little later the bottle has become 'bottles'. Cf. iv. i. 207.

126. kiss the book. Stephano hands Trinculo the bottle. He is referring to the custom, still surviving in courts of law, of kissing the Bible when taking an oath.

137. thy dog, and thy bush. The Man in the Moon was supposed to carry a bush on his back, and to have a dog going before him. In the Mechanicals' play in *A Midsummer Night's Dream* (v. i. 137) the character who represents Moonshine comes on 'with lanthorn, dog, and bush of thorn'.

141. I afeard of him! The effect of the liquor on Trinculo is to give him some 'Dutch courage'. Caliban, on the other hand, grows excited, and thinks of gaining his freedom from Prospero, even though he does so by serving Stephano instead.

154. But that &c. Trinculo is completing his previous speech.

166. marmozet: the name nowadays of a small monkey found only in South America. But the word was in use before America was discovered.

168. [scamels. The word is not found elsewhere, and the commonest explanation is that the 'scamels' of the Folio is a mistake for 'sea-mells', i.e. sea-mews, or sea-gulls. Many other emendations have been put forward. In Strachey's *True Repertory* mention is made of 'a kind of webb-footed Fowl . . . of the bigness of an English green Plover, or Sea-Mew . . . which birds for their blindness (for they see weakly in the day) and for their crying and whooting, we called the Sea Owl'.]

171. Here; bear my bottle. It is not clear whether it is to Caliban or Trinculo that he is entrusting the bottle.

174. A howling monster. . . . Coleridge notes 'the delight of Trinculo at finding something more sottish than himself and that honours him—the characteristic of base and vulgar minds which Shakespeare is fond of lashing and placing in a ridiculous light'.

175. **No more dams.** 'When Raleigh's first governor of Virginia,
Ralph Lane, detected in 1586 signs of hostility among the natives
about his camp, his thoughts at once turned to the dams or weirs.
Unless the aborigines kept them in good order, starvation was a
certain fate of the colonists, for no Englishman knew how to con-
struct and work these fish-dams, on which the settlement relied for
its chief sustenance. . . . Caliban's threat to make "no more dams
for fish" exposed Prospero to a very real and familiar peril.' (Sir
Sidney Lee.)

179. **Ca—Caliban:** possibly intended to indicate a hiccup.

ACT III. Scene I

The drunken voice of Caliban having died away in the distance, the
stage is left empty for a few moments and then the King's son enters
'bearing a log'. The gentle events of this scene—'the most beautiful
love-scene in Shakespeare' (Quiller-Couch)—contrast with the
drunken orgy of the previous one. The unseen Prospero, hovering
approvingly in the background, is the embodiment of a benign
Providence.

1–4. **There be some sports . . . ends:** i.e. 'Some sports demand
much effort, but the delight removes the sense of labour; it is noble
to endure some kinds of base employment, and very unimportant
duties have valuable results'—'sets off' = 'removes'. But 'sets
off' may mean 'acts as a foil to', like a setting to a jewel, in which
case Ferdinand is saying, 'The labour involved in them sets off (i.e.
heightens) the delight.'

15. **Most busy lest . . . it.** The reading given is that of the Folio.
There have been many emendations, but the meaning comes
through in much the same way to all readers; viz. 'I am forgetting
my task; but these sweet thoughts of Miranda make my labours
light, and really I am busiest when I seem least busy'—i.e. when
he forgets his task, and his mind is busied with thinking about
Miranda. 'Lest' is another form of 'least', and 'lest (or least)
when I do it' = 'when I am working least'—the word 'it' referring
loosely to 'my labours'.

> [The following list of emendations will illustrate how this famous crux
> has been tackled: 'Most busy least'; 'Least busy'; 'Most busyless';
> 'Most busiest'; 'Most busy left when idlest'.]

19. **'Twill weep . . . you:** a 'conceit'. Shakespeare is perhaps thinking of the green wood burning, and the moisture coming out of the

log. Trees which exude gum or resin are said to 'weep'. Cf. Milton, *Paradise Lost*, iv. 248: 'Groves whose rich trees wept odorous gums and balm.'

23–5. If you'll sit down, . . . pile. 'It is by selecting such little and almost imperceptible circumstances that Shakespeare has more truly painted the passions than any other writer: affection is more powerfully expressed by this simple wish and offer of assistance, than by the unnatural eloquence and witticisms of Dryden, or the amorous declamations of Rowe.' (Joseph Warton.)

31. Poor worm! Besides its more common contemptuous use, 'worm' was used in Shakespeare's day as an expression of tenderness, more particularly of lovers.

32. visitation: a word regularly used for the plagues which 'visited' Elizabethan London. Shakespeare may have that meaning in his mind—i.e. the 'infection' of love has visited Miranda—but perhaps he is thinking only of Miranda's visit to Ferdinand in the cell.

37. Admir'd Miranda! Shakespeare is playing on the literal meaning of the name 'Miranda', viz. 'the woman that must be admired'.

48–9. I do not know . . . sex. But cf. I. ii. 46–7.

51. More that I may call men. Miranda has apparently considered Caliban, and deliberately rejected him as ineligible for the name of 'man'.

61. I would not so! i.e. 'Would I were not a king but only a prince still, for then my father would be still alive.'

84. your maid. Perhaps Shakespeare intended two meanings to be read into this word: (1) unmarried girl, (2) servant.

89. here's my hand. This action of the lovers in plighting their troth by shaking hands, however strange to-day, seems to have been a normal procedure in Elizabethan times. Cf. *The Winter's Tale*, I. ii. 103–4,

> Ere I could make thee open thy white hand,
> And clap thyself my love.

92–3. So glad . . . withal. The lovers are gladder than he (1) because their happiness is heightened by surprise. (Prospero is certainly glad, but he knew what was coming.); or (2) because it is *their* love—they are overwhelmed with it.

[**surpris'd.** This word may carry its usual meaning of 'taken unawares'. But in Elizabethan English it might mean 'seized with (an emotion)', or even 'overpowered'.]

ACT III. Scene II

Some time has elapsed since we last saw Caliban and his new friends: we could tell that if only because they have all grown drunker in the interval. In this scene a conspiracy is hatched against Prospero—a grotesque parody of that against Alonso and Gonzalo. Ariel's dartings about the stage contrast strikingly with the lurching clumsiness of the drunken sailors and Caliban. The scene closes with Prospero apparently in danger of being assassinated.

2–3. bear up, and board 'em : a sailor's phrase used in attacking an enemy vessel. Stephano is thinking of another attack on the bottle. It is as if an intoxicated character in a modern play should say, 'Up guards, and at 'em!'

4. the folly of this island! This may be merely a humorous reflection of the drunken Trinculo, viz. 'What a mad place this island is!', or he may be proposing a toast to be drunk.

> [Taking the exclamation in this second sense, Dover Wilson makes the ingenious emendation: 'The Sophy of this island!' The 'Sophy' was the Shah of Persia; and Trinculo, if this interpretation is accepted, is proposing a toast to Stephano.]

9. set. Trinculo is punning on this word, of course. Stephano has just used it to describe the fixed, glazed appearance of a drunkard's eyes.

14. [Thou shalt . . . monster. The Folio reads 'Lieutenant Monster', without the comma. In view of the 'Servant-Monster' above we should perhaps read 'Lieutenant-Monster' here.]

16. standard. Trinculo puns again; i.e. Caliban is so drunk that he cannot stand up.

43. Thou liest. Here the purely mischievous side of Ariel's character appears. Cf. Puck in *A Midsummer Night's Dream*, ii. i. 32–57. The interruptions of Ariel must be heard on the stage to be appreciated: the effect is almost one of ventriloquism. Caliban thinks that Trinculo spoke.

58. the party. The word 'party' is no longer used of an individual except in a facetious sense; e.g. 'a stout old party'. In Elizabethan English it was still possible to use it quite seriously.

60. Where . . . a nail into his head. Caliban's brutality is well illustrated by the method he proposes of dispatching Prospero. Cf. iii. ii. 86–9. It was Jael's way with Sisera. See Judges iv. 18–21. Shakespeare knew his Bible.

62. **pied ninny.** Trinculo is a jester, and as such he will be wearing the fool's motley. Similarly, 'patch' refers to the fool's patch-like clothes.

69. **stock-fish.** The point of Stephano's threat is that, in the process of being dried, cod were thoroughly beaten.

81-2. [**Prithee stand further off.** These words are generally taken as having been addressed to Trinculo. But it is possible that Shakespeare was thinking of Caliban, and that the actor who originally took Stephano's part went through some vulgar clowning to show that it was Caliban's 'ancient and fish-like smell' that prompted the remark.]

94. **utensils.** This word was accented on the first syllable. Its meaning here is vague: perhaps 'household effects'. Caliban's 'for so he calls them' may be Shakespeare's way of apologizing for making the ignorant Caliban use such a word at all. Cf. ll. 97-8: 'he himself Calls her a nonpareil.'

99. **dam.** See note to i. ii. 373

115. **catch:** a part-song in which one singer 'catches up' the words that another has just sung, and proceeds to sing them again as the first proceeds to the second line.

117. **do reason:** give you satisfaction. This phrase was also used among drinking companions with the sense of drinking the health of some one.

119. [Folio has 'Flout 'em and cout 'em: and skowt 'em and flout 'em'. 'Cout' (a dialect form of 'colt' = 'befool') may be the right reading. (Dover Wilson.)]

120. **Thought is free.** The phrase seems to have become proverbial. It occurs again in *Twelfth Night*, where Maria says to Sir Andrew, 'Now, sir, thought is free' (i. iii. 74).

123-4. **the picture of Nobody.** An anonymous comedy, published some time before *The Tempest* was written, called *Nobody and Somebody*, contained a print showing a figure of *Nobody*. The figure has only head, arms, and legs—no body. It is doubtful, however, if this print could have been familiar enough to Shakespeare's audience to enable them to understand the reference. More probably Shakespeare is alluding to the sign over the shop of John Trundle, a bookseller and publisher of ballads. Trundle published 'at his Shop in the Barbican, at the Signe of No-body'.

126. **take 't as thou list.** Either 'take what shape you please'; or 'take my remark as you like'.

132–140. Be not afeard &c. Caliban may be brutal, but compared to the prosaic and sophisticated Stephano and Trinculo he shows natural feeling, and in such a speech as this he adds remarkably to the poetic impression made by the play.

144. I remember the story: i.e. what you have just told me about Prospero. Or is it the story of the maiden who counted her chickens before they were hatched?

149. [Wilt come? . . . Stephano. The words 'Wilt come?' are given by most modern editors to Stephano, and Trinculo is then made to say, 'I'll follow, Stephano.' In the Folio, however, the whole speech is given to Trinculo, and printed as in our text. Trinculo must be supposed to be addressing Caliban, who is presumably standing there irresolutely: 'Will you come? I'm going to follow Stephano.']

ACT III. Scene III

In this scene—a very spectacular one with its dancing shapes, its thunder and lightning, and its vanishing banquet—nemesis falls at last on the evil-doers. Their punishment is pronounced, but their ultimate fate is kept in suspense, for two more Acts have still to come.

s.d. *on the top.* At this point Prospero would appear in the gallery or upper stage (see p. 20). The 'several strange Shapes' are, of course, below, on the main stage. Shakespeare's audience would not demand to be told just where Prospero was supposed to be; it was enough that he was 'above', and wearing his invisible cloak.

23. phoenix: a fabulous bird of Arabia. It lived for 600 years, and when it began to grow old it built itself a nest of sweet-smelling twigs on which to die. From the body of the dead bird there was born a new phoenix. There was never more than one alive at a time.

32. [gentle-kind. Folio has 'gentle, kinde', i.e. gentle and kind, which may be the correct reading.]

39. Praise in departing: a proverbial expression, meaning, 'Don't praise too soon', i.e. 'Wait till the end before giving your praise, lest you should have reason to retract it.'

45. Dew-lapp'd like bulls. The dewlap is the fold of loose skin hanging from the necks of cattle and some other animals. The 'mountaineers' are most probably Swiss peasants, who, in certain districts of the Alps, are still afflicted with goitre. The physical appearance of this complaint is more or less accurately described by Gonzalo's words.

46–7. men Whose heads . . . breasts. These never existed outside a traveller's tale. In 1595 Sir Walter Raleigh sailed to South America on a voyage of discovery and in his account of the expedition mentioned 'a nation of people, whose heads appeare not above their shoulders; which though it may be thought a meere fable, yet for mine owne part I am resolved it is true. . . . They are reported to have their eyes in their shoulders, and their mouthes in the middle of their breasts.' In *Othello* (I. iii. 144–5) Shakespeare had already referred to

> men whose heads
> Do grow beneath their shoulders.

48. Each putter-out of five for one. It was common among Elizabethan travellers to 'speculate' on their safe return. The traveller 'put out' or 'put forth' a certain sum of money when he set out, and if he returned alive he reaped a handsome profit. One rate which seems to have been offered—though surely only on very exceptional risks—was £5 for every £1 paid down. Cf. Jonson, *Every Man out of his Humour*, II. i. 'I am determined to put forth some five thousand pound, to be paid me five for one, upon the return of myself, my wife, and my dog from the Turk's court at Constantinople.' It will be noticed that in this queer form of Elizabethan insurance one did not insure against accident, but gambled on one's safety. The speculator, in fact, did not put out five for one, but one for five, i.e. he was a putter out *at the rate of* five for one.

49–52. stand to . . . The *O.E.D.*, citing this passage, gives the meaning as 'to set to work, fall to; esp. to begin eating'. But perhaps Alonso means only, 'I will approach the table; . . . take your stand with me, and do as I do'. The 'we' here is probably the royal 'we', used by a king when speaking in public of himself.

s.d. *harpy.* The harpy was a fabulous monster, with a woman's face and the wings and claws of a bird, often sent by the gods to torment mortals. In Virgil's *Aeneid*, Book iii, Aeneas describes how he and his followers are driven by storms to the islands where the harpies dwell. Every time that they sit down to eat, the harpies come beating their wings and snatching at the food.

s.d. *a quaint device.* From a stage direction later in this scene it appears that the 'quaint device' extended only to the disappearance of the food and wine. The table itself is afterwards carried out by the 'shapes'. The most probable explanation is that the stage carpenter had constructed a table with a false top.

53–6. whom Destiny . . . you. The 'you' is redundant. Some editors emend 'you' to 'yea, . . .'.

58–60. I have made you mad . . . selves. Soon afterwards Alonso talks of suicide (100–2); and Antonio and Sebastian are desperate men, ready to fight the legions of the fiends (102–3).

62. whom. 'In almost all cases where *who* refers to an irrational antecedent [i.e. not a person], an action or personal feeling is implied, so that *who* is the subject. *Whom* is rare.' (Abbott.)

61–6. the elements . . . invulnerable. In the *Aeneid*, Book iii, Aeneas and his friends determine to drive off the harpies by force; but their weapons are powerless against these terrible creatures. In Phaer's translation of the *Aeneid* (1558), which Shakespeare probably knew, the fight with the harpies is described in the following words:

> Their swords by them they laid . . .
> And on the filthy birds they beat . . .
> But fethers none do from them fal, nor wound nor strok doth bleed,
> Nor force of weapons hurt them can.

66. [like invulnerable. The Folio punctuation here is 'like-invulnerable'.]

80. falls: cf. Appendix II, 'Verbs', p. 183.

84. a grace . . . devouring: i.e. a devouring grace. To 'devour with the eyes' is to gaze upon with avidity. This is probably the idea that Shakespeare means to convey here. The word may have been suggested to him by its appropriateness to a harpy: the harpies were always pictured as rapacious and greedy, and the removal of the food was a sort of devouring of it. Dover Wilson suggests 'devoiring' = 'serving', 'waiting at table'.

86. with good life. 'Life' here may be either 'liveliness', or 'life-likeness'. In the second sense we still use the phrase, 'to the life'.

90. distractions. The three victims of Prospero's magic are all left stupefied, rooted to the spot. Gonzalo's question to Alonso, 'Why stand you in this strange stare?' indicates the distracted condition of the King.

92. whom. Two separate constructions are combined, viz. 'who they suppose is drown'd', and 'whom they suppose to be drown'd'.

95–103. The different reactions of Alonso on the one hand, and of Sebastian and Antonio on the other, are important in the further development of the play. The first repents, and his repentance makes a happy ending possible; the other two are hardened in their villainy, and remain callous to the end.

ACT IV. Scene I

In this scene—again a spectacular one—the process of reconciliation between Prospero and his enemies begins. Ferdinand, the son of his old enemy, is accepted by Prospero for his son-in-law. Caliban, however, still remains to be punished along with his two new friends. Again the blundering entrance of Stephano and his party provides a striking contrast with what has just gone before.

1-8. If I have . . . gift. The milder Prospero now reappears. If he were to continue much longer to act as the stern avenging power he would lose the sympathy of the audience.

3. third. Prospero's life has been bound up in three people—his daughter, his wife, himself. But his wife is dead, and Miranda is now, as he says himself, 'that for which I live'. Others suggest that the three parts of Prospero's life are himself, his dukedom, and his daughter. Or, again, he may mean that he has still got a third part of his life left to live; but since he lives now only for Miranda he is giving away that final third.

[Some editors change third to 'thrid', i.e. 'thread'.]

9. [boast her off. Most probably 'off' is an intensive adverb, used on the analogy of 'set off', i.e. 'to the best advantage'. Folio has 'boast her of', perhaps for 'boast of her'. Folio 2 has 'her off'. Dover Wilson emends to 'hereof', and takes the word as referring to Prospero's rich gift.]

18. aspersion. The word was used of the sprinkling of water at religious ceremonies, notably at baptisms. The idea of 'slander', 'calumny' (i.e. a sprinkling or bespattering with what soils or stains) is a slightly later development of the meaning.

21. weeds. The marriage bed was normally strewn with flowers.

23. Hymen's lamps. Hymen was the god of marriage. He was generally represented as holding a blazing torch in his hand. Cf. *infra*, l. 97.

30-1. When I shall think . . . below. Ferdinand, longing on his wedding-day for night to fall, will wonder how the sun can take so long to set. This idea is represented by two images: either the steeds of Phoebus, the charioteer of the sun, must have gone lame, or else Night has been chained under ground, and cannot appear to take the place of day.

33. What, Ariel! Prospero is simply summoning Ariel, not uttering an exclamation of surprise.

37. **rabble:** swarm, medley. The word was not invariably used in Shakespeare's day with a contemptuous significance, though here it may be.

56. **liver.** The liver was supposed to be the seat of love and passion.

59. **No tongue! all eyes!** The words are addressed to Ferdinand and Miranda. One had to keep silence at an incantation, or else the charms would fail.

s.d. IRIS: one of the messengers of the gods, more particularly of Juno. She represented the rainbow in Greek mythology, and therefore always appeared with multi-coloured wings. Cf. *infra* 70–1, 76.

60–138. The masque, with its set speeches in rhyming couplets, is at once more formal and more simple than the broken, conversational blank-verse dialogue that precedes it.

60. **Ceres:** the goddess of corn and harvests, the daughter of Saturn and Vesta.

64. **pioned and twilled.** The meaning of those two adjectives is uncertain. 'Pioned' has been variously explained as 'trenched', 'peonied' (i.e. with peonies), &c. For 'twilled' numerous emendations have been put forward, e.g. 'lilied', 'tulip'd', 'tilled', 'willow'd'.

66. **[broom groves.** 'Broom' has been queried by some editors on the ground that broom hardly grows high enough to afford shade. 'Brown' has been suggested in place of 'broom', but though a printer might set up 'brown' instead of 'broom', he is unlikely to have substituted 'broom' for 'brown'.]

69. **thy sea-marge.** Sicily was supposed to be the favourite retreat of Ceres.

74. **her peacocks.** Peacocks were Juno's attendant birds. They drew her car through the sky.

79. **honey-drops:** honey-dew, the nectar found in flowers. The old belief was that the honey-dew on flowers fell from the sky in the same way as the ordinary dew was thought to fall on the grass.

82. **Rich scarf.** The rainbow is thought of as a scarf worn by the earth as an adornment.

85. **some donation.** It has been suggested by W. J. Lawrence that the 'donation' here referred to was an actual gift made by the performers of the masque to the betrothed couple in honour of whom this masque was written. (Cf. Introduction, pp. 8, 15.) Such presentations were not uncommon. When, therefore, Juno says (l. 103) 'Go with me' she probably steps forward with Iris and Ceres to present the gift or gifts.

89. dusky Dis. Pluto, King of Hades (hence 'dusky') carried off Proserpina, the daughter of Ceres, to his kingdom under the earth, and made her his queen. Cf. Milton, *Paradise Lost*, iv. 268–71.

> . . . . that fair field
> Of Enna, where Proserpine gathering flowers,
> Herself a fairer flower, by gloomy Dis
> Was gather'd, which cost Ceres all that pain . . .

93. Paphos: a town in the island of Cyprus particularly devoted to the worship of Venus.

94. Dove-drawn. Doves were the favourite birds of Venus, and are always represented as drawing the chariot of the goddess of love.

s.d. *Juno descends.* She was probably let down from above by some machine.

103. sister. Juno and Ceres were both daughters of Saturn.

114–15. Spring . . . harvest. The surface meaning here seems to be, 'May spring follow for you immediately after harvest', i.e. 'May there be no winter in your lives, only Spring, Summer, and harvest time'. But 'spring' may be taken to have the additional sense of 'offspring'. Juno has just called on Ceres to go with her and bless Ferdinand and Miranda that they may be 'honour'd in their issue'. 'Spring' here is clearly a veiled reference to the 'off-spring' of the royal marriage, since nine months from the beginning of 1613 takes us to 'the very end of harvest' (Dover Wilson).

119. charmingly. Shakespeare is probably thinking of Prospero's charms which have produced the vision. The meaning would therefore be 'magically', though the more usual sense 'delightfully' may also have been present in his mind.

123–4. So rare . . . Paradise. If, as has often been suggested, *The Tempest* was performed as part of the festivities following upon the betrothal of Elizabeth, daughter of James I, to the young Elector Palatine, this passage would almost inevitably be interpreted as a compliment to James.

[In some copies of the Folio the reading is 'wise', in others it is 'wife'.]

124–5. Sweet, now, . . . seriously. These words, it has been suggested, belong to Miranda. Prospero calls for silence because otherwise the spell would not hold. Cf. l. 59.

128. Naiades: female deities who presided over the rivers, springs, wells, and fountains.

128. windring. The word is not found apart from this passage. 'Windring' may be a misprint for 'winding' or 'wandering', but Shakespeare may have coined an expression by combining both.

s.d. *heavily*: i.e. sorrowfully. Shakespeare obviously expects his audience to connect the gloomy disappearance of the nymphs and reapers with Prospero's sudden recollection of Caliban's treachery. Their alteration from cheerfulness to gloom prepares the way for the reappearance of evil in the play.

148–56. Our revels now are ended ... behind. Many critics insist upon seeing in this passage Shakespeare's farewell to the stage; but such an idea is probably no more than the baseless fabric of a somewhat sentimental vision. The lines have been regarded as an 'undramatic expression of his own sentiments', but in their context they are entirely dramatic, and require no secondary meaning to give them significance.

151. baseless: i.e. without a base, or foundation, immaterial.

152–6. [The cloud-capp'd towers ... behind. These famous lines appear to owe something to a passage in *The Tragedy of Darius*, by William Alexander, Earl of Sterling, which was published in 1603:

> Let greatnesse of her glascie scepters vaunt;
> Not sceptours, no, but reeds, soone brus'd soone broken:
> And let this worldlie pomp our wits inchant.
> All fades, and scarcelie leaves behinde a token.
> Those golden Pallaces, those gorgeous halles,
> With fourniture superfluouslie faire:
> Those statelie Courts, those sky-encountring walles
> Evanish all like vapours in the aire.]

164. Come with a thought! ... come! Prospero, catching sight of Ariel, exclaims, 'Come with a thought!' i.e. 'I was just thinking about you, and here you are!' The second 'come' is his command to Ariel to follow him. 'I thank thee' is most probably addressed to Ariel; but many editors, holding that these three words are spoken to Ferdinand and Miranda, in acknowledgement of 'We wish your peace', change 'thee' to 'you' or 'ye', and alter the punctuation.

[The most recent emendation (by Dover Wilson) is very ingenious, viz. 'I think thee, Ariel', i.e. 'I *think* you to me, I have only to think and you come'.]

179. lowing. Ariel's words are not, of course, to be taken literally. The 'lowing' here is the sound of his tabor, and just as calves will follow the mooing of the herd, so these men followed the sound of the drum.

182. filthy-mantled. The 'mantle' is the green coating on a stagnant pool. Cf. *Lear*, III. iv. 136–7: 'Poor Tom, that ... drinks the green mantle of the standing pool.'

184. O'erstunk. It has been pointed out that the feet of Caliban and his friends, being at the bottom of the pool, could hardly be offensive. This is an objection only if we take 'o'erstunk' as = 'made to stink all over'. There is no difficulty if we interpret 'stank worse than'.

my bird: cf. 'My Ariel, chick'. (v. i. 316.)

187. stale: a decoy bird, i.e. a living or stuffed bird used for the purpose of enticing other birds into a net.

193. line. The commentators are divided as to whether the line on which the apparel is hung is a clothes-line or a linden, or line tree, the older form of 'lime'. (Cf. 'line-grove', v. i. 10.) Property trees do appear to have formed part of Elizabethan stage scenery; e.g. in *The Spanish Tragedy* Hieronimo's son is hanged on a tree in full view of the audience. A clothes-line is certainly the natural line on which to hang clothes. The fact that it is less 'poetical' than a linden tree is irrelevant here, for the scene is broad comedy.

205. hoodwink: blindfold, cover up with a hood so as to prevent one from seeing. Hawks were regularly covered with a hood or cap when they were not being flown at game.

221. king Stephano. Trinculo is alluding to an old ballad, *King Stephen was a worthy peer*. Two stanzas of this ballad are sung in *Othello* (II. iii. 92).

230. [Let's along. Folio has 'Let's alone'. Shakespeare may have written 'Let's all on'. (Dover Wilson.)]

235. jerkin: a garment for the upper part of the body, a close-fitting jacket, jersey, or short coat, often made of leather. Here it seems to be made of fur, or undressed skin. (Cf. 'You are like to lose your hair', l. 236.)

under the line: (1) under the clothes-line, (2) at the equator. The meaning of this passage would be clearer if we knew just how Stephano acted at this point. Perhaps he takes the jerkin off the clothes-line, and it is then 'under the line'. In saying that the jerkin is 'like to lose' its 'hair', he may be alluding to the loss of hair that follows upon fevers contracted in hot climates, i.e. 'under the line', at the equator.

237. **Do, do**: a puzzling and, in the context, pointless remark, unless
it refers back to Stephano's 'Be you quiet, monster'.

> [Folio has 'Doe, doe'. Two alternative suggestions are that the words
> are equivalent to 'That will do', or that Trinculo's teeth are chattering
> with cold. Cf. *Lear*, III. iv. 57–8. 'Tom's a-cold. O! do de, do de, do de'.]

241–2. **pass of pate**: 'pass' = the thrust in fencing; 'pate' = head.

243. **put some lime . . . fingers.** Trinculo is alluding to the
custom of catching birds by smearing branches with bird-lime.
Bird-lime is very sticky: Trinculo therefore suggests facetiously
that Caliban should put some on his fingers, so that the rest of the
apparel may stick to them.

246. **barnacles**: wild geese. These were supposed to be produced
from the barnacle shell. (Barnacles are the small marine creatures
found clinging to the timbers of a ship or to other solid objects.)
Caliban is clearly alluding to geese here, and not to barnacle shells.
From geese he goes on naturally to think of apes.

s.d. *A noise of hunters heard,* &c. The hunting of the conspirators
by the spirit hounds may be regarded as an 'anti-masque', i.e. a
comic masque after the serious one which has preceded it. In the
anti-masques performed at Court the masquers frequently appeared
as animals, e.g. goats, bears, monkeys. (A. H. Thorndike.)

254. **Silver!** One of the dogs mentioned in *The Taming of the Shrew*
(I. i. 19) is called Silver, which suggests that 'Mountain', 'Fury',
and 'Tyrant' were also names commonly given by the Elizabethans
to their dogs.

257. **dry convulsions.** The meaning of 'dry' here is perhaps the
same as that in the phrase 'dry beating'. A 'dry' beating was one
that caused a bruise but did not draw blood, a severe, stiff beating.

261. [Lie. Folio has 'Lies', which may be what Shakespeare wrote. Cf.
I. i. 15, and Note.]

ACT V. Scene I

This final act is devoted to Prospero's various dealings with those that
have wronged him. Alonso, now repentant, is forgiven; Sebastian
and Antonio are forgiven, but rebuked; Stephano and his two companions have already been punished, but now they are exposed to
their masters. Ferdinand and Miranda receive the blessing of Alonso,
and all is well again with Prospero.

2. **crack not.** Prospero's charms 'hold'. Shakespeare may be thinking of a magician's glass or alembic without a flaw, or 'crack' may
carry on the metaphor of a boil or ulcer from the previous line.

3. **Goes upright . . . carriage.** 'Carriage' is probably the burden
that Time is carrying. Time is not bowed down under his burden,
but is walking upright, and therefore briskly. Prospero's plans,
therefore, are 'well up to time'.

24. **Passion:** probably a verb here, but it may be a noun, the object
of 'relish'.

27–8. **the rarer action . . . vengeance:** 'it is a finer thing to be
virtuous than to take vengeance'. 'Virtue' conveys the idea of a
goodness which rises superior to all thoughts of personal revenge.

33–50. **Ye elves . . . art.** Shakespeare was here indebted to Arthur
Golding's translation of a passage in Ovid's *Metamorphoses*, vii.
197–206:

> Ye Ayres and windes: ye Elves of Hilles, of Brookes, of Woods alone,
> Of standing Lakes, and of the Night . . .

Golding has 'whole woods and Forestes I remove: I make the
Mountaines shake'; 'I call up dead men from their graves'; 'Our
Sorcerie dimmes the Morning faire'; 'Among the Earthbred
brothers you a mortall war did set', &c.

35. **the ebbing Neptune:** here, of course, the sea. Shakespeare is
remembering how children will run after the ebbing wave, and then
as quickly run back when it flows in again, so as not to wet their
feet.

37. **green sour ringlets.** Prospero is alluding to the circles of darker
grass often found in meadows; they are popularly supposed to be
formed by the fairies dancing in a ring, and so called 'fairy rings'.
The ewe 'not bites' those ringlets because the grass is rank and
sour.

40. **the solemn curfew.** The curfew bell was still rung regularly in
towns and villages in Shakespeare's day, usually at the hour of
eight or nine in the evening. The fairies 'rejoice to hear it' because
the sound tells them that mortals will soon be abed, and the hour
of their revels is close at hand.

41. **Weak masters.** The fairies are 'weak masters', because though
they have *some* mastery over the elements their supernatural power
amounts to very little.

45. **Jove's stout oak.** The oak was sacred to Jupiter; it was he who
first taught men to live upon acorns. He is usually represented in
ancient art holding some of his thunderbolts in his hand.

53. **that:** 'whom', the antecedent being implied in 'their'. Or, alternatively, the antecedent of 'that' may be 'To work mine end upon their senses', in which case 'that' = 'which'. Prospero is saying (1) 'To work my end upon the senses of those for whom . . .', or (2) 'To work my end upon their senses, which is what this airy charm is for'.

54. **I'll break my staff.** Here again many readers of *The Tempest* interpret those words as Shakespeare's veiled announcement that he intends to write no more for the stage. But this announcement of Prospero's is dramatically important in view of the widespread distrust of magic in Shakespeare's day. However benevolently Prospero has used his powers, he has nevertheless been dabbling in forbidden practices, and his promise here to 'drown his book' is an assurance that he means to give them up. Shakespeare was not in the way of 'signing' his plays, or introducing scraps of personal information for his future biographers. But those who believe that Shakespeare is using Prospero here to take his own personal farewell of play-writing will continue to believe so; it is not a matter of fact, but of intuition.

s.d. *circle.* Prospero has traced a circle on the ground with his magic staff. Those who enter that circle are in his power.

58. **and the best comforter.** The force of 'and' here is almost 'which is'.

59. **fancy:** imagination.

60. [**boil'd.** Folio has 'boile', which may be retained if (*a*) 'which' is understood before 'now useless', or (*b*), 'boile' is interpreted as 'like a boil, or tumour'.]

64–8. **The charm . . . reason:** a striking example of the metaphorical way in which Shakespeare's mind works. In quick succession he passes from 'dissolves' to 'steals', 'melting', 'rising', 'chase', 'mantle'.

67. **mantle.** This word was used of the creamy scum that forms over fermenting liquors. Cf. 'rising senses', 'fumes'.

79–82. **Their understanding . . . muddy.** This whole passage is remarkably dramatic. The audience is looking on at the strange recovery of the enchanted lords: the effect is that of men slowly regaining consciousness after being drugged. The bare acting of it would be impressive: with Prospero's commentary it is doubly so. The image of an estuary with the tide out seems to have kept recurring to Shakespeare while he was writing this play. Cf. I. i. 53–4; II. i. 221, and the repetition of the words 'ooze', 'oozy', 'mudded'.

88–94. [**Where the bee sucks. . . .** 'Theobald would make Ariel say "there lurk I" and "after sunset" instead of "there suck I" and "after summer", and Arne has popularized both these emendations. The second change was made because the bat hibernates, a fact of natural history of which the dramatist was supposed to be unaware. . . . The mention of the bat indicates, as Theobald said, that Ariel rode after sunset, but it is also meant to imply . . . that he rode in pursuit of summer, for summer was his season of activity, just as it is the bat's. We may waive the fact that the bat was not a migratory creature; drama does not pretend to expound natural history with scientific exactitude, and, moreover, the island on which Ariel lived was not one where nature existed in its usual order.' (R. Noble.)]

96. so, so, so. Prospero apparently utters these words as he is putting on his hat and buckling on his rapier.

100. enforce. The word used by Prospero is vague, and no doubt intentionally so. Ariel is to transport the mariners to Prospero's cell, but just how he is to do so is left undefined.

105. Inhabits: cf. I. i. 15, &c.

124. subtilties. This word had various meanings in Elizabethan English which it has now lost: e.g. (a) stratagem, deception, (b) 'a highly ornamental device, wholly or chiefly made of sugar, sometimes eaten, sometimes used as a table decoration'. In view of the word 'taste' in the previous line, and the mock banquet of Act III, scene iii, Shakespeare has apparently the second meaning in his mind, but is probably thinking of the first as well. Prospero is telling the lords that they are still experiencing some subtle effects of the island, i.e. the illusions they have witnessed.

126. brace. The word 'brace' is used here to express contempt.

127. his highness' frown: i.e. Alonso's anger. Prospero could, if he cared, disclose how Sebastian and Antonio had plotted against the King's life.

146. means much weaker. Alonso has still his daughter Claribel left, and she will comfort him for the loss of his son. Prospero had only one child, a daughter, and now she is gone.

150. The king and queen there!: an example of dramatic irony. Ferdinand and Miranda are not yet in Naples, nor king and queen there, but some day, as the audience know—though Alonso does not—they will be.

156. [**their words.** Dover Wilson reads 'these words', i.e. the words spoken by Prospero. The lords, in fact, think he is a spirit, not a human being.]

167. look in. At this point, or immediately after, the curtains that separate the inner from the outer stage are drawn apart.

174. score. The meaning may be (*a*) twenty or (*b*) an account, what is scored up. In either case Miranda is saying that whatever Ferdinand does she will call it right. 'Wrangle' means 'to contend', 'to dispute stubbornly', and so 'to argue out of possession'.

176–7. one dear son . . . lose. Alonso is so sure that this is no vision but actually his son, that if it does prove to be a vision after all he will have all the grief of losing his son a second time.

178–9. Though the seas . . . cause. Ferdinand has just looked up, and, to his astonishment, seen that his father is still alive.

183–4. O brave new world . . . in't! These words are absolutely natural to Miranda, who has been brought up in ignorance of all mankind except her father, and who now sees Alonso and the lords in their magnificent clothes. Shakespeare brings out her innocence without making her too innocent. A lesser dramatist would either have omitted her surprise altogether, or else exaggerated it.

219. That swear'st grace o'erboard. The boatswain's swearing is so terrible that he drives all grace (the grace of God) overboard.

223. three glasses. Cf. 'three hours' (l. 186). The frequency with which Shakespeare makes his characters allude to the duration of the action in this play makes it appear as if he himself were unusually conscious of it. In *The Tempest*, whether consciously or not, the 'three unities' of neo-classical criticism are for once observed by Shakespeare. The time of the action is confined, as Aristotle required, to a single revolution of the sun; the scene of the action is the same throughout, viz. the island; and the action itself is one and entire, viz. the revenge of Prospero.

236. [in all her trim. Folio reads 'in all our trim'. This may be the correct reading, if the boatswain is referring to the fact mentioned in Act I, scene ii, and Act II, scene i that the clothes of the shipwrecked company were undamaged by the salt water. R. E. C. Houghton suggests: 'at liberty | Were we in all our trim; freshly beheld. . . .']

    freshly. It is the 'royal, good, and gallant ship' that is fresh. The epithet has been transferred to the verb.

238. Capering. The master was jumping about with delight to see his ship safe. The word is often applied to the motion of a ship itself, and Shakespeare may have been thinking of that when he used it of the master.

248. [Which shall be shortly, single . . . Folio reads '(Which shall be shortly single)'. If we retain this punctuation 'single' must be taken as 'complete', i.e. Prospero's leisure will soon be unbroken.]

249. Which to you . . . probable. Prospero assures Alonso that once he has heard the explanation of how these strange events happened they will no longer appear strange.

253. Untie the spell. Prospero had previously spoken of his enemies 'all knit up in their distractions' (III. iii. 89–90).

256. Every man shift . . . rest. Stephano is still, of course, fuddled, and is presumably mixing up his words. 'Let every men shift for (take care of) himself' is, of course, the usual expression.

258. bully-monster. For the use of 'bully' here, cf. 'bully Bottom' in *A Midsummer Night's Dream*.

261. brave spirits. Caliban takes Alonso and the rest for another manifestation of spirits called up by Prospero. Anything nobler than himself he thinks a god or a spirit. It will be remembered that he took Stephano for a god.

267. badges. Prospero is referring to the stolen apparel, which reveals the dishonesty of Stephano and Trinculo, who would normally be wearing Alonso's badge to indicate that they were in his service.

270. makes flows and ebbs. Tides are caused by the 'pull' of the moon on the earth.

272. demi-devil. Cf. I. ii. 319–20. Caliban's father was a devil, though his mother was not. Caliban is therefore half a devil.

279. reeling-ripe. Liquor is said to be ripe when it is mature, and the word is extended to the person who has drunk the liquor, i.e. ripe till he is reeling about. The modern equivalent would be 'mellow'.

283–4. I shall not fear fly-blowing. Meat that has been pickled is in no danger of being fly-blown.

286–7. a cramp. Stephano is one big ache all over.

310. retire me. The verb is used reflexively.

317. That is thy charge. Ariel's last charge is to see that auspicious gales are blowing, and that the sea is calm.

318. Please you, draw near. Perhaps the company gathers behind Prospero in a semicircle while he speaks the Epilogue. But more probably he is motioning them towards his cell, and the actors go off through the inner stage. The outer stage, it will be remembered, had no curtain.

Epilogue. Prospero now addresses the audience, half as Prospero still, half as the actor who has played the part of Prospero. But again certain readers believe that in the Epilogue Shakespeare is speaking of himself, and that when Prospero talks of being sent to Naples or being 'here confin'd by you' Shakespeare is weighing the possibility of his own retirement to Stratford-on-Avon or of remaining in London. With this interpretation in mind, all sorts of phrases take on a personal significance, e.g. 'my charms are all o'erthrown' = 'I have given up writing plays, and am now only an ordinary citizen.' His 'dukedom' is (presumably) enough money saved to retire upon, but what fanciful interpretation can be put upon 'the deceiver' it is hard to say. Whether there is any likelihood that Shakespeare was making a veiled reference to his retirement in the Epilogue (and we do not even know for certain that *The Tempest* was his last play), Prospero's words have a quite satisfactory surface meaning:—'I am no longer Prospero, the powerful magician, for I have broken my magic staff. I am now a humble actor in *your* hands, waiting for your applause to let me leave the stage and join my fellow actors. So now that you have watched the play and seen me recover my dukedom, please let me go off the stage ("this bare island"). Release me with your applause ("the help of your good hands"). If I don't succeed in obtaining your cheers ("gentle breath", &c.), our play has failed, for we aimed at pleasing you. I can't *compel* approval now because I've abjured my magic; I can now only pray you to be merciful to the faults of actors and play—otherwise I shall be left in despair. As you would have your own sins forgiven, so in your indulgence give me liberty to go.'

All through the Epilogue Prospero is almost putting himself in the position of his own Ariel; he is some one bound to serve the public, and the public is able to free him as he freed Ariel. He carries on, too, the idea of magic and spells.

10. **With the help ... hands.** Cf. IV. i. 124–7. The clapping of hands, by suddenly breaking the silence, would snap the spell. Latin comedies ended with the word 'Plaudite', i.e. applaud, clap your hands. This epilogue of Shakespeare's is only an elaboration of that one word. It should be compared with the epilogue spoken by Puck in *A Midsummer Night's Dream*, and that spoken by Rosalind in *As You Like It*.

15. **despair.** Here probably Shakespeare is thinking of the desperate end to which necromancers must come unless prayer to God saves their souls in time. Faustus in his extremity cries to his friends, 'Ay, pray for me, pray for me'. (Warburton.)

17–18. **Which pierces ... faults:** i.e. which pierces the air to reach the mercy seat of God, and wins pardon for all our sins.

SELECT LITERARY CRITICISM

The Tempest

The Tempest is one of the most original and perfect of Shakespeare's productions, and he has shown in it all the variety of his powers. It is full of grace and grandeur. The human and imaginary characters, the dramatic and the grotesque, are blended together with the greatest art, and without any appearance of it. Though he has here given 'to airy nothing a local habitation and a name', yet that part which is only the fantastic creation of his mind has the same palpable texture, and coheres 'semblably' with the rest. As the preternatural part has the air of reality, and almost haunts the imagination with a sense of truth, the real characters and events partake of the wildness of a dream. . . . Even the local scenery is of a piece and character with the subject. Prospero's enchanted island seems to have risen up out of the sea ; the airy music, the tempest-tossed vessel, the turbulent waves, all have the effect of the landscape background of some fine picture. Shakespeare's pencil is (to use an allusion of his own) 'like the dyer's hand, subdued to what it works in'. Everything in him, though it partakes of 'the liberty of wit', is also subjected to 'the law' of the understanding. For instance, even the drunken sailors, who are made reeling-ripe, share, in the disorder of their minds and bodies, in the tumult of the elements, and seem on shore to be as much at the mercy of chance as they were before at the mercy of the winds and waves.

From W. HAZLITT, *Characters of Shakespeare's Plays* (1817).

The Tempest, among Shakespeare's later plays, is a counterpart to the *Midsummer Night's Dream* of his lyric youth. Here, too, is a dream, or, if you will, a fairy tale, in which the protagonists are not men and women but imagined beings, taken partly from folk-belief and partly from literature, to be the symbols of forces dimly perceived by the poet as ruling that life, which is itself, after all, in another degree, but such stuff as dreams are made on. And, like *A Midsummer Night's Dream*, the play must interest the spectator less through a strictly

dramatic appeal to his emotions, than by the strange romantic
charm of its setting and its sensuous realization of the delicate
and the grotesque in the mysterious personages which it brings
before him. It is, in fact, to be classed as dramatic *spectacle*
rather than as drama proper, and the elaboration with which it
has been put upon the stage by modern managers may be
regarded as not, in this case, wholly out of keeping with the
intention of the dramatist.

> From E. K. CHAMBERS, Preface to *The Tempest*, in
> Red Letter Shakespeare (1904).

The Contemporary Significance of the Play

WHILE then the drama before us is apparently so remote in
locality and detail from Virginia, it is most curious to observe
how many of the topics brought up by colonies and colonization
are indicated and characterized in the play.—The wonders of
new lands, new races; the exaggerations of travellers, and their
truths more strange than exaggeration; new natural pheno-
mena, and superstitious suggestions of them; the perils of the
sea and shipwrecks; the effect of such fatalities in awakening
remorse for ill deeds, not unremembered because easily committed; the quarrels and mutinies of colonists for grudges new
and old, the contests for authority of the leaders, and the greedy
misdirection of industry while even subsistence is precarious;
the theories of government for plantations, the imaginary and
actual characteristics of man in the state of nature, the com-
plications with the indigenae, the resort, penally or otherwise, to
compelled labour, the reappearance on new soil of the vices of
the older world, the contrast of moral and intellectual qualities
between the civilized and the savage, and the gradual appre-
hension of the wondrous strangers by the savage . . . all these
topics, problems, and conjunctures came up in the plantation of
Virginia by James I; and familiarity with them . . . would
heighten the sensibility of the audience to every scene.

> From W. W. LLOYD, *Critical Essay* to Singer's *Shakespeare* (1856).

The day of warring armies and revengeful ghosts was passing,
but the audiences' craving for novelty was unceasing, and it is
amply cared for . . . in *The Tempest*. *The Tempest*, to us a

beautiful poem full of beneficent idealism, on the Elizabethan stage must have seemed largely an effort to satisfy this craving. Caliban, that immensely taking Elizabethan stage-beast, who has proved so prophetically philosophical, must have been the hit of the play. Then there was the old device borrowed from the *Midsummer Night's Dream* of the invisible Ariel bewildering the courtiers, and the still older business of the vanishing banquet, 'accomplished with a quaint device'. Then there were the drunken scenes, such as Shakespeare had used before, but now made especially diverting when the climax was reached and the dogs chased the drenched and filthy boors about the stage, while Prospero and Ariel cried on quarry! Prospero him self, with his magician's robes and wand, must have made an imposing spectacular figure.

From A. H. THORNDIKE, *The Influence of Beaumont and Fletcher on Shakespeare* (1901).

The playwright, least of all craftsmen, can pursue his art along fixed and unvarying lines. He must be alert to perceive changes in the public taste, he must be conscious of the value of novelty, he must study the successes and the failures of his fellows. As he grows in maturity and insight, he must put the best of his ripened powers into his work. If he fails to do these things, he will soon find himself falling behind, and becoming, not the entertainer of the present, but the memory of a bygone generation. Shakespeare made no such mistake. He was singularly quick to perceive changes in theatrical fashions, to provide his public with new varieties of amusement, and to pour out the best which he had to give for their deeper reflection. This was characteristic of him down to the very end of his active career in the theatre. In the *Tempest*, perhaps the last play wholly from his pen, he adapted effective elements from the Court masques and from current tales of adventure in the New World, which were then stirring the imagination of Englishmen, with no hint of the fatigue or the indifference of the magician about to break his staff and drown his book.

From W. W. LAWRENCE, *Shakespeare's Problem Comedies* (1931).

The Construction of the Play

ENCHANTMENT is a thing wholly outside our experience, it has
no associations of memory interweaved with it, nor has it ever
appealed to our sympathies in real life. The artist who drama-
tizes a supernatural story is perpetually facing the practical
difficulty—how to bridge over the gulf between his supernatural matter and the experience of his hearers or readers.
There are three modes of treatment open to a dramatist by
which he may meet such a difficulty. First, he may *derationalize*,
or remove as far as possible from commonplace experience, the
general surroundings amidst which the supernatural is to
appear. Again, he may *rationalize* the supernatural element itself, that is, give it as many points of contact as possible with
thought and experience. Yet again, he may give further support to the supernatural element by uniting with it as much as
possible of what is nearest akin to it in the world of reality. All
three modes of treatment are combined in Shakespeare's handling of Enchantment in the present play. . . .

The very scene, insulated like a magic circle, is excluded from
the commonplace, and is confined to that remoteness of nature
in which distance from the real presents itself as nearness to the
unseen. On the enchanted island there is nothing to break the
spell by a suggestion of every-day experience, and the atmosphere is electrical with enchantment; while the inhabitants,
untouched by social influences, are formed equally by nature
and magic. As the story moves before us, the laws of nature—
the basis of our sense of reality—appear suspended, and it is the
unnatural which presents itself as a thing of law. When at last
personages of familiar experience are introduced, they fall
wholly under the mysterious influence, and their realism—their
tender loving and brutal carousing—only serves to remind us
how much of real life is permeated by Enchantment.

From R. G. MOULTON, *Shakespeare as a Dramatic Artist* (1888).

In handling enchantment one point of art will be to mark the
process of passing from the real to the supernatural. . . . Shakespeare's play recognizes only a single transition stage between
reality and enchantment—music, strangely linked with dreamy
slumber. . . . The sleepy atmosphere seems a fixed quality of

the climate, dulling the critical faculty that might question the
visionary appearances. The music, however, that breaks out
from time to time is always an immediate herald of some supernatural effect: it is through this gate alone that we pass out into
the world of enchantment.

Ibid.

Just here, however, comes in the dramatist's difficulty.
Shakespeare is henceforth occupied, and to the end, with
reconciliation. But (as I have pointed out) reconciliation, forgiveness, the adjustment and restoration of goodwill between
injured and injurer must be, in the nature of things, a slow process. And this, of all themes, is the most heartbreaking for a
dramatist, who has to tell, and by presented action, his complete story in two or three hours. Again and again this difficulty beat Shakespeare; and on our way through the later plays
we have seen the devices by which he covered defeat. . . . And
then of a sudden, in *The Tempest* Shakespeare brings off the
trick! The whole action of the play, with the whole tale of
ancient wrong unfolded, the whole company of injuring and
injured gathered into a knot, the whole machinery of revenge
turned to forgiveness, takes place in about three hours of
imagined time, or just the time of its actual representation on
the stage!

'Marvellous stage craft?' Yes. I would not make too much
of the famous Unities, but though discredited as *laws*, they
abide as *graces* of drama; and pre-eminently a grace is this
Unity of Time, whereby the author in Dryden's words—

sets the audience, as it were, at the post where the race is to
be concluded; and, saving them the tedious expectation of
seeing the poet set out and ride the beginning of the course,
suffers you not to behold him till he is in sight of goal and just
upon you.

From ARTHUR QUILLER-COUCH, *Shakespeare's Workmanship* (1918)

The Supernatural Element

THAT the character and conduct of Prospero may be understood,
something must be known of the system of enchantment which
supplied all the marvellous found in the romances of the Middle

Ages. This system seems to be founded on the opinion that the fallen spirits, having different degrees of guilt, had different habitations allotted to them at their expulsion, some being confined to Hell, some, as Hooker, who delivers the opinion of our poet's age, expresses it, 'dispersed in air, some on earth, some in water, others in caves, dens, or minerals under the earth'. Of these some were more malignant and mischievous than others. The earthy spirits seem to have been thought most depraved, and the aerial the least vitiated. Thus Prospero observes of Ariel,

> —Thou wast a spirit too delicate
> To act her *earthy* and abhorred commands.

Over these spirits a power might be obtained by certain rites performed or charms learned. This power was called the Black Art, or knowledge of enchantment. The enchanter being, as King James observes in his *Demonology*, one who commands the Devil, whereas the witch serves him. Those who thought best of this art, the existence of which was, I am afraid, believed very seriously, held that certain sounds and characters had a physical power over spirits, and compelled their agency; others who condemned the practice, which in reality was surely never practised, were of opinion, with more reason, that the power of charms arose *only* from compact, and was no more than the spirits voluntarily allowed them for the seduction of man. The art was held by all, though not equally criminal, yet unlawful, and therefore Casaubon, speaking of one who had commerce with spirits, blames him, though he imagines him 'one of the best kind who dealt with them by way of command'. Thus Prospero repents of his art in the last scene. The spirits were always considered as in some measure enslaved to the enchanter, at least for a time, and as serving with unwillingness; therefore Ariel so often begs for liberty, and Caliban observes that the spirits serve Prospero with no good will, but hate him rootedly. —Of these trifles enough.

From S. JOHNSON, *The Plays of William Shakespeare* (1765).

The delineation of Prospero, the noblest conception of the *Magic* character which ever entered the mind of a poet, is founded upon a distinction which was supposed to exist between the several professors of this mysterious science. They were separated, in fact, into two great orders: into those who commanded the service of superior intelligences, and into those who, by voluntary compact, entered into a *league with*, or submitted to be the *instruments* of lower powers. Under the first were ranked *Magicians*, who were again classed into higher or inferior, according to the extent of the control which they exerted over the invisible world; the former possessing an authority over *celestial*, as well as infernal spirits. Under the second were included Necromancers and Wizards, who, for the enjoyment of temporary power, subjected themselves, like the Witch, to final perdition.

Of the highest class of the first order was Prospero, one of those Magicians or Conjurors who, as Reginald Scot [author of *The Discoverie of Witchcraft*, 1584] observes, 'professed an art which some fond divines affirme to be more honest and lawfull than *necromancie*, which is called *Theurgie*; wherein they work by good angels'. Accordingly, we find Prospero operating upon inferior agents, upon elves, demons, and goblins, through the medium of Ariel, a spirit too delicate and good to 'act abhorr'd commands', but who 'answered his best pleasure', and was subservient to his 'strong bidding'.

Shakespeare has very properly given to the exterior of Prospero several of the adjuncts and costume of the popular magician. Much virtue was inherent in his very garments; and Scot has, in many instances, particularized this fashion. A pyramidal cap, a robe furred with fox-skins, a girdle three inches in breadth, and inscribed with cabalistic characters, shoes of russet leather, and unscabbarded swords formed the usual dress.

From N. DRAKE, *Shakespeare and his Times* (1817).

The Style of 'The Tempest'

SHAKESPEARE mingles everything, he runs line into line, embarrasses sentences and metaphors; before one idea has burst its shell, another is hatched and clamorous for disclosure.

From C. LAMB, *Specimens of the English Dramatic Poets* (1808).

The style of these last plays is a further development of the style of the Tragedies. The thought is often more packed and

hurried, the expression more various and fluent, at the expense
of full logical ordering. The change which came over Shakespeare's later work is that which Dryden, at an advanced age,
perceived in himself. 'What judgment I had', he says in the
Preface to the *Fables*, 'increases rather than diminishes; and
thoughts, such as they are, come crowding in so fast upon me,
that my only difficulty is to choose or to reject, to run them into
verse, or to give them the other harmony of prose.' The bom-
basted magniloquence of the early rhetorical style has now dis-
appeared. The very syntax is the syntax of thought rather than
of language; constructions are mixed, grammatical links are
dropped, the meaning of many sentences is compressed into one,
hints and impressions count for as much as full-blown proposi-
tions. An illustration of this late style may be taken from the
scene in *The Tempest*, where Antonio, the usurping Duke of
Milan, tries to persuade Sebastian to murder his brother
Alonso, and to seize upon the kingdom of Naples. Ferdinand,
the heir to the kingdom, is believed to have perished in the shipwreck, and Antonio points to the sleeping king:

Antonio. Who's the next heir of Naples?
Sebastian.   Claribel.
Antonio. She that is Queen of Tunis; she that dwells
            Ten leagues beyond man's life . . .

        [Raleigh quotes the next seven lines—ii. i. 240–9.]

Here is a very huddle of thoughts, tumbled out as they present
themselves, eagerly and fast. This crowded utterance is not
proper to any one character; Leontes in his jealous speculations,
Imogen in her questions addressed to Pisanio, Prospero in his
narrative to Miranda, all speak in the same fashion, prompted
by the same scurry of thought. It would be right to conclude,
from the mere reading, that there was no blot in the papers to
which these speeches were committed.

The later style of Shakespeare, as it is seen in the Tragedies
and Romances, is perhaps the most wonderful thing in English
literature. From the first he was a lover of language, bandying
words like tennis-balls, adorning his theme 'with many holiday
and lady terms', proving that a sentence is but the cheveril
glove to a good wit, so quickly the wrong side may be turned

outward. He had a mint of phrases in his brain, an exchequer of words; he had fed of the dainties that are bred in a book; his speech was a very fantastical banquet. This early practice gave him an assured mastery, so that when his thoughts multiplied and strengthened, he was able to express himself. There has never been a writer who came nearer to giving adequate verbal expression to the subtlest turns of consciousness, the flitting shadows and half-conceived ideas and purposes which count for so much in the life of the mind—which determine action, indeed, although they could not be rationally formulated by a lawyer as a plea of action. His language, it is true, is often at its simplest when the thought is most active. . . . But where the situation allows of it, Shakespeare's wealth of expression is bewildering in its flow and variety. Ideas, metaphors, analogies, illustrations, crowd into his mind, and the pen cannot drive fast enough to give them full expression. He tumbles his jewels out in a heap, and does not spend labour on giving to any of them an elaborate setting. 'His mind and hand went together', but his mind went the faster.

From W. RALEIGH, Shakespeare (1907).

The Songs in 'The Tempest'

As to the last two plays we have no difficulty as to date; we have fairly strong evidence that both *The Winter's Tale* and *The Tempest* were first produced in 1611. The songs therein contained are therefore the final development. Both contain a new kind of action song—set songs so deeply embedded in the text as dialogue that it is unnecessary to stop the action to permit them to be performed, for they are essentially a part of it. Had we possessed no information as to the dates of the two plays, there would even then have been no hesitation in assigning a late date to all the songs of Autolycus and Ariel.

From R. NOBLE, Shakespeare's Use of Song (1923).

Shakespeare and 'The Tempest'

OF dramatic action in the stricter sense of the term there is little or none; for the action is throughout, down to its smallest details, planned and ordered by Prospero. He is the magician—one might almost go further and say the playwright—and the other figures are his puppets. This peculiar character of Prospero's has gone far in its unconscious influence towards creating the belief that Prospero is in effect Shakespeare himself, that we can hear in *The Tempest* Shakespeare speaking in his own voice rather than giving speech to a dramatic creation. . . . There is much, certainly, towards the end of the play, to suggest this view and impress it on us; and with due caution, it may be largely accepted. It is based not only on the epilogue; not only on Prospero's announcement of his own purpose to

> retire me to my Milan, where
> Every third thought shall be my grave;

not only on the earlier passage where he orders Ariel to intro-duce the masque of goddesses and the dance of nymphs and reapers, with the curious soliloquizing words:

> I must
> Bestow upon the eyes of this young couple
> Some vanity of mine art: it is my promise,
> And they expect it from me;

though, indeed, 'my Milan' we must inevitably think of as Stratford, and 'this young couple' as the new generation. Nor is it only in that marvellous passage—the most famous as it is the most magnificent in all Shakespeare if not in all literature—beginning 'Our revels now are ended'. . . . Not only in those concluding scenes, but more subtly throughout, Prospero is, as I have suggested, the playwright; controlling, evolving, sus-pending, varying, interrupting, or resuming the action; the other characters, though alive with the full Shakespearian vitality, being, so far as concerns their action, figures that move at Prospero's manipulation. The dramatist has projected him-self bodily into the drama. For once, and for once only, he lets us see him actually at work. It is perhaps this double conscious-ness—as though we were simultaneously in front watching the play as spectators, and behind seeing it being handled—that makes *The Tempest* not in fact . . . . highly effective on the stage. The illusion or hallucination to which, in seeing a play acted, we are asked to abandon ourselves, has not its full chance. But when we read it, if we read it carefully enough, it brings us nearer than almost anything else to understanding Shakespeare's art. It gets us closer to Shakespeare himself than we are likely to come by other means, whether by building insubstantial fabrics of arbitrary hypothesis, by searching in the plays for theories or obsessions, or by extracting from them revelations about Shakespeare's own experiences.

From J. W. MACKAIL, *The Approach to Shakespeare* (1930).

I believe that *Measure for Measure* and *The Tempest* are Shakespeare's greatest plays of forgiveness.

From R. W. CHAMBERS, *The Jacobean Shakespeare and 'Measure for Measure'* (1937).

The Tempest was probably his last play—in the sense, at least, that he designed it for his farewell to the stage. The thought which occurs at once to almost every reader of the play, that Prospero resembles Shakespeare himself, can hardly have been absent from the mind of the author. . . . In all the work of Shakespeare there is nothing more like himself than those quiet words of parting—'Be cheerful, sir; our revels now are ended'.

From W. RALEIGH, *Shakespeare* (1907).

But as Shakespeare never wholly enters into his characters, as in every case only a part of his personality is contained in them, we cannot regard Prospero as an embodiment or symbolization of Shakespeare merely because his ripeness and serenity of mind may possibly reflect a part of Shakespeare's nature as it was at that time. It is surely an amazing piece of irony that critics seek to discover the greatest humorist the world has ever known precisely in that creation of his genius which is the least gifted with a sense of humour.

From L. L. SCHÜCKING, *Character Problems in Shakespeare's Plays* (1922).

Yet I cannot believe that there is any allegory, or symbolism, or even 'veiled biography' here. *The Tempest,* like every other Shakespearian or popular Elizabethan drama, stands like a tub on its own bottom, is a story in its own right and for its own

sake; and unless the intention of the author be of no primary
importance, and meanings be not derived from the text but imparted to it, this must be only a rather simpler story of his than
usual, a sort of glorified fairy-tale on the stage, precious, not
indeed because of the structure or situations, but because of the
characters, the poetry, and the rich and dreamy spirit which for
the most part informs it. That the story is slight is no proof that
there is another within or behind it. And Prospero is not Shakespeare any more than (as fewer think) he is James I. . . . Ariel
is not genius, or the lawless imagination, craving liberty but
kept in servitude; Miranda is not the drama; Caliban, not the
vulgar public; Milan, not Stratford; and the enchanted isle, not
the stage, or London, or the world. . . . Not only do I think such
an interpretation unwarranted by the text and the spirit of the
poet, I think it actually troubles and disturbs the artistic effect.

Above all this is true of the characters, especially the mythical
ones most eagerly seized upon as symbols—Ariel and Caliban.
Where does the beauty or greatness of these creations lie if not
in their reality? They are not single abstractions personified,
but many-sided conceptions incarnated. They are not spirits
such as are to be found in Shelley's verse dramas, but beings more
actual and convincing than Miranda and Ferdinand themselves.

From E. E. STOLL, *The Tempest*, *P.M.L.A.*, vol. xlvii (1932).

Shakespeare's Last Plays

A COMPARISON naturally suggests itself, between what was perhaps the latest of Shakespeare's completed works, and that
early drama which first gave undoubted proof that his imagination had taken wings. The points of resemblance between *The
Tempest* and *A Midsummer Night's Dream*, their common atmosphere of romance and magic, the beautiful absurdities of their
intrigues, their studied contrasts of the grotesque with the
delicate, the ethereal with the earthy, the charm of their lyrics,
the *verve* of their vulgar comedy—these, of course, are obvious
enough; but it is the points of difference which really make the
comparison striking. One thing, at any rate, is certain about
the wood near Athens—it is full of life. The persons that haunt
it—though most of them are hardly more than children, and

some of them are fairies, and all of them are too agreeable to be true—are nevertheless substantial creatures, whose loves and jokes and quarrels receive our thorough sympathy; and the air they breathe—the lords and the ladies, no less than the mechanics and the elves—is instinct with an exquisite good-humour, which makes us as happy as the night is long. To turn from Theseus and Titania and Bottom to the Enchanted Island, is to step out of a country lane into a conservatory. The roses and the dandelions have vanished before preposterous cactuses, and fascinating orchids too delicate for the open air; and, in the artificial atmosphere, the gaiety of youth has been replaced by the disillusionment of middle age. Prospero is the central figure of *The Tempest*; and it has often been wildly asserted that he is a portrait of the author—an embodiment of that spirit of wise benevolence which is supposed to have thrown a halo over Shakespeare's later life. But, on closer inspection, the portrait seems to be as imaginary as the original. To an irreverent eye, the ex-Duke of Milan would perhaps appear as an unpleasantly crusty personage, in whom a twelve years' monopoly of the conversation had developed an inordinate propensity for talking. These may have been the sentiments of Ariel, safe at the Bermoothes; but to state them is to risk at least ten years in the knotty entrails of an oak, and it is sufficient to point out, that if Prospero is wise, he is also self-opiniated and sour, that his gravity is often another name for pedantic severity, and that there is no character in the play to whom, during some part of it, he is not studiously disagreeable. But his Milanese countrymen are not even disagreeable; they are simply dull. 'This is the silliest stuff that e'er I heard', remarked Hippolyta of Bottom's amateur theatricals; and one is tempted to wonder what she would have said of the dreary puns and interminable conspiracies of Alonzo, and Gonzalo, and Sebastian, and Antonio, and Adrian, and Francisco, and other shipwrecked noblemen. At all events, there can be little doubt that they would not have had the entrée at Athens.

The depth of the gulf between the two plays is, however, best measured by a comparison of Caliban and his masters with Bottom and his companions. The guileless group of English mechanics, whose sports are interrupted by the mischief of Puck, offers a strange contrast to the hideous trio of the 'jester', the 'drunken butler', and the 'savage and deformed slave', whose designs are thwarted by the magic of Ariel. Bottom was the first of Shakespeare's masterpieces in characterization, Caliban was the last: and what a world of bitterness and horror lies between them!

From LYTTON STRACHEY, *Books and Characters* (1922).

The remaining three plays of the traditional Shakespeare canon exhibit an altered mood, a kindlier and happier view of man's life and character. It is true, as Mr. Lytton Strachey has pointed out, that there are no worse characters anywhere than Iachimo and others, and that these plays are full of hideous crimes. But when he makes this a ground for questioning the 'serenity' of Shakespeare's final outlook, the answer is simple. These last plays end on a new note. The crimes do not triumph as they do in the tragedies. They fail. And the criminals are forgiven. The final word is no longer mere acquiescence in fate; it is forgiveness, reconciliation, recovery, peace. And the curtain falls now on life, not on death. In the tragedies those for whom we have most cared—Othello, Desdemona, Brutus, Hamlet and Ophelia, Lear and Cordelia—all die at or before the end of the play. Now they all live. If they have died or seemed to die, they are miraculously restored to life. The sins of the stupid— a Cymbeline, a Leontes—are not now irretrievable or repented in vain. The end is atonement: the lost are found, the estranged are reconciled, the quarrelling fathers and daughters, husbands and wives, whose quarrels have made the play, end it by becoming one family again.

From JOHN BAILEY, *Shakespeare* (1929).

The Characterization in the Play

THE leading characters are not merely typical, but symbolical— that is, they do not illustrate a class of persons, they belong to universal nature. Consider the scene of the play. Shakespeare is wont to take some familiar story, to lay his scene in some place the name of which, at least, is familiar—well knowing the reserve of power that lies in the familiar as a background, when things are set in front of it under a new and unexpected light. But in the *Tempest* the scene is laid nowhere, or certainly in no country laid down on any map. Nowhere, then? At once nowhere and anywhere—for it is in the soul of man, that still vexed island hung between the upper and the nether world, and liable to incursions from both. There is scarce a play of Shakespeare's in which there is such variety of character, none in which character has so little to do in the carrying on and development of the story. But consider for a moment if ever the Imagination has been so embodied as in Prospero, the Fancy as in Ariel, the brute Understanding as in Caliban, who, the moment his poor wits are warmed with the glorious liquor of Stephano, plots rebellion against his natural lord, the higher Reason. Miranda is mere abstract Womanhood, as truly so before she sees Ferdinand as Eve before she was wakened to consciousness by the echo of her own nature coming back to her. the same, and yet not the same, from that of Adam. Ferdinand, again, is nothing more than Youth, compelled to drudge at something he despises, till the sacrifice of will and abnegation of self win him his ideal in Miranda. The subordinate personages are simply types: Sebastian and Antonio, of weak character and evil ambition; Gonzalo, of average sense and honesty; Adrian and Francisco, of the walking gentlemen who serve to fill up a world. They are not characters in the same sense with Iago, Falstaff, Shallow, or Leontes.

From J. R. LOWELL, *Among My Books* (1870).

Thus strangely remote is the world of Shakespeare's latest period; and it is peopled, this universe of his invention, with beings equally unreal, with creatures either more or less than human, with fortunate princes and wicked step-mothers, with goblins and spirits, with lost princesses and insufferable kings. And of course, in this sort of fairy land, it is an essential condition that everything shall end well; the prince and princess are bound to marry and live happily ever afterwards, or the whole story is unnecessary and absurd; and the villains and goblins must naturally repent and be forgiven. But it is clear that such conventional closes to fantastic tales, cannot be taken as evidences of serene tranquillity on the part of their maker; they merely show that he knew, as well as any one else, how such stories ought to end. . . . In *The Tempest* unreality has reached its apotheosis. Two of the principal characters are frankly not human beings at all; and the whole action passes, through a series of impossible occurrences, in a place which can only by courtesy be said to exist. The Enchanted Island, indeed, peopled, for a timeless moment, by this strange fantastic medley of persons and of things, has been cut adrift for ever from common sense, and floats, buoyed up by a sea, not of waters, but of poetry.

From LYTTON STRACHEY, *Books and Characters* (1922).

The Character of Prospero

ARIEL is swayed more by fear than gratitude, a fact which excites Prospero's anger. And here let it be remarked what necessities belong to dramatic characterization. Although Shakespeare would not exhibit Prospero with his clear spiritual will and power obscured and turmoiled by the sensual appetites and passions that made the lives of Antony and Cleopatra 'a storm whereon they rode'; yet, had he depicted his benevolent magician as basking perpetually in the sunshine of an open conscience and uninterruptedly serene, we should have had a being elevated so far above the condition of humanity that we could not have sympathized with him. He therefore presents him as chafed with certain obstacles in the magic sphere of his working, and as occasionally wroth with Ariel and Caliban for resistance expressed or implied. He is also liable to perturbation of mind from forgetfulness, as in the Fourth Act, when he suddenly remembers the conspiracy of Caliban. And thus, with all his moral excellence, Prospero is made to awaken our sympathy for a natural imperfection.

From J. A. HERAUD, *Shakespeare—His Inner Life* (1865).

The Character of Miranda

IT is the peculiar excellence of Shakespeare's heroines, that they seem to exist only in their attachment to others. They are pure abstractions of the affections. We think as little of their persons as they do themselves, because we are let into the secrets of their hearts, which are more important. We are too much interested in their affairs to stop to look at their faces, except by stealth and at intervals. No one ever hit the true perfection of the female character, the sense of weakness leaning on the strength of its affections for support, so well as Shakespeare: no one ever so well painted natural tenderness free from affectation and disguise: no one else ever so well showed how delicacy and timidity, when driven to extremity, grow romantic and extravagant; for the romance of his heroines (in which they abound) is only an excess of the habitual prejudices of their sex, scrupulous of being false to their vows, truant to their affections, and taught by the force of feeling when to forego the forms of propriety for the essence of it. His women were in this sense exquisite logicians; for there is nothing so logical as passion. They knew their own minds exactly; and only followed up a favourite purpose, which they had sworn to with their tongues, and which was engraven on their hearts, into its untoward consequences.

From W. HAZLITT, *Characters of Shakespeare's Plays* (1817).

In the very first speech of Miranda the simplicity and tenderness of her character are at once laid open; it would have been lost in direct contact with the agitation of the first scene. . . . In Shakespeare all the elements of womanhood are holy, and there is the sweet yet dignified feeling of all that *continuates* society, as sense of ancestry and of sex, with a purity unassailable by sophistry. . . . Shakespeare saw that the want of prominence, which Pope notices for sarcasm ['Most women have no character at all'], was the blessed beauty of the woman's character, and knew that it arose not from any deficiency, but from the more exquisite harmony of all the parts of the moral being constituting one living total of head and heart. He has drawn it, indeed, in all its distinctive energies of faith, patience, constancy, fortitude,—shown in all of them as following the heart, which gives its results by a nice tact and happy intuition, without the intervention of the discursive faculty, sees all things in and by the light of the affections, and errs, if it ever err, in the exaggerations of love alone.

From S. T. COLERIDGE, *Lectures on Shakespeare* (1818).

I would suggest to the reader's consideration the curious
felicity of the scene where Ferdinand and Miranda acknowledge
their affection to each other. I mean in the harmonious contrast
between a young prince, bred in a Court, himself the centre of a
sphere of the most artificial civilization, and a girl, not only
without any knowledge of the world and society, but even without previous knowledge of the existence of any created man but
her father and Caliban.—Brought up in all but utter solitude,
under no influence but that of her wise and loving father on
earth and her wise and loving Father in Heaven, Miranda
exhibits no more coyness in her acceptance of Ferdinand's over-
tures than properly belongs to the instinctive modesty of her
sex, unenhanced by any of the petty, pretty arts of coquetry
and assumed shyness, which are the express result of artificial
female training. The simple emotion of bashfulness, indeed,
which (in spite of her half-astonished, half-delighted exclamation—'Do you love me?' that elicits her lover's passionate
declaration) causes her 'to weep at what she's glad of', is so
little comprehensible to herself, that she shakes it off with
something like self-reproach as an inviolable disingenuousness:
'Hence, bashful *cunning*'; and then with that most pathetic
and exquisite invocation to 'plain and holy innocence' offers her
life to her lover with the perfect devotion and humility of the
true womanly nature. In the purity and simplicity of this
'tender of affection', Ferdinand made acquaintance with a
species of modesty to which assuredly none of those ladies of the
Court of Naples 'whom he had eyed with best regard' had ever
introduced him.

From MRS F A. KEMBLE, *Notes upon Some of Shakespeare's*
Plays (1882).

The Character of Stephano

BUT Trinculo's recognition-scene with Stephano (Caliban being
used in it with the funniest plausibility) makes capital farce;
and Stephano himself is, I dare to say, a master-stroke of invention. I may be thought to speak extravagantly here, for his
share in the action is not of first-rate importance. But let us
consider his value in contributing *solidarity* to our trust in a

play which throughout the artist had to watch against its becoming too ethereal, too pure and good

> for human nature's daily food,

and floating off into sheer phantasy. But an unmistakable
British seaman turned loose to stagger through our isle of magic,
with a bottle!—The scheme wanted but that: a priceless British
mariner, staggering through all but to stare, and against Ariel's
fine-drawn melodies hiccoughing back—

> The master, the swabber, the bo'sun, and I . . .

Truly I see the beginnings of what they call 'our world-wide
empire' in Stephano. Let the reader mistake me not: I see
them also in Andrew Marvell's mariners, rowing, 'where the
remote Bermudas ride', and chanting

> In the English boat
> A holy and a cheerful note.

But I detect them also in this unholier drunken figure, be-
wildered, yet positive that all is to be risked.—

> I escaped upon a butt of sack, which the sailors heav'd o'erboard
> . . . Tell not me! When the butt is out we will drink water: not a
> drop before.

That, with his immortal advice in extremity, 'Every man shift
for all the rest', gives the man's measure.

From ARTHUR QUILLER-COUCH, Shakespeare's
Workmanship (1918).

The Character of Ariel

IF a doubt could ever be entertained whether Shakespeare was
a great poet, acting upon laws arising out of his own nature,
and not without law, as has sometimes been idly asserted, that
doubt must be removed by the character of Ariel. The very
first words uttered by this being introduce the spirit, not as an
angel, above man; not a gnome, or a fiend, below man; but
while the poet gives him the faculties and the advantages of
reason, he divests him of all moral character, not positively, it
is true, but negatively. In air he lives, from air he derives his
being, in air he acts; and all his colours and properties seem to

have been obtained from the rainbow and the skies. There is nothing about Ariel that cannot be conceived to exist either at sun-rise or at sun-set: hence all that belongs to Ariel belongs to the delight the mind is capable of receiving from the most lovely external appearances. His answers to Prospero are directly to the question, and nothing beyond; or where he expatiates, which is not infrequently, it is to himself and upon his own delights, or upon the unnatural situation in which he is placed, though under a kindly power and to good ends. . . .

Is there anything in nature from which Shakespeare caught the idea of this delicate and delightful being, with such child-like simplicity, yet with such preternatural powers? He is neither born of heaven, nor of earth; but, as it were, between both, like a May-blossom kept suspended in air by the fanning breeze, which prevents it from falling to the ground, and only finally, and by compulsion, touching earth. This reluctance of the sylph to be under the command even of Prospero, is kept up through the whole play, and in the exercise of his admirable judgement Shakespeare has availed himself of it, in order to give Ariel an interest in the event, looking forward to that moment when he has to gain his last and only reward—simple and eternal liberty.

From s. t. coleridge, *Lectures on Shakespeare* (1811–12).

The Character of Caliban

To return once more to Shakespear; no man ever drew so many characters, or generally distinguished 'em better from one another, excepting only Johnson [i.e. Ben Jonson]: I will instance but in one, to show the copiousness of his invention; 'tis that of Caliban, or the monster in *The Tempest*. He seems there to have created a person which was not in Nature, a boldness which at first sight would appear intolerable; for he makes him a species of himself, begotten by an Incubus on a Witch; but this, as I have elsewhere prov'd, is not wholly beyond the bounds of credibility, at least the vulgar still believe it. . . . Whether or no his generation can be defended, I leave to Philosophy; but of this I am certain, that the Poet has most judiciously furnish'd him with a person, a language, and a character which will suit him both by Father's and Mother's side: he has all the discontents and malice of a Witch, and of a Devil; besides a convenient proportion of the deadly sins; Gluttony, Sloth, and Lust are manifest; the dejectedness of a slave is likewise given him, and the ignorance of one bred up in a Desart Island. His person is monstrous, . . . and his language is as hobgoblin as his person; in all things he is distinguished from other mortals.

From J. DRYDEN, *Preface to 'Troilus and Cressida'* (1679).

The character of Caliban is wonderfully conceived; he is a sort of creature of the earth, as Ariel is a sort of creature of the air. He partakes of the qualities of the brute, but is distinguished from brutes in two ways:—by having mere understanding without moral reason; and by not having the instincts which pertain to absolute animals. Still, Caliban is in some respects a noble being; the poet has raised him far above contempt; he is a man in the sense of the imagination: all the images he uses are drawn from Nature and are highly poetical; they fit in with the images of Ariel. Caliban gives us images from the earth, Ariel images from the air.

From S. T. COLERIDGE, *Lectures on Shakespeare* (1811–12).

[Shakespeare] peoples the air with sportive fawns and sylphs; and these beings, existing only in imagination, possess such truth and consistency, that even when deformed monsters, like Caliban, he extorts the assenting conviction, if there should be such beings they would so conduct themselves.

From A. W. SCHLEGEL, *Lectures on Dramatic Literature*, trans. by John Black (1815).

Caliban is malicious, cowardly, false, and base in his inclinations; and yet he is essentially different from the vulgar knaves of a civilized world, as they are occasionally portrayed by Shakespeare. He is rude, but not vulgar; he never falls into the prosaic and low familiarity of his drunken associates, for he is a poetical being in his way; he always speaks in verse. He has picked up everything dissonant and thorny in language, out of which he has composed his vocabulary; and of the whole variety of nature, the hateful, repulsive, and pettily deformed have alone been impressed on his imagination.

Ibid.

These fellows [Stephano and Trinculo] with their sea-wit are the least to our taste of any part of the play: but they are as like drunken sailors as they can be, and are an indirect foil to Caliban, whose figure acquires a classical dignity in the comparison. The character of Caliban . . . is the essence of grossness, but there is not a particle of vulgarity in it. Shakespeare has described the brutal mind of Caliban in contact with the pure and original forms of nature; the character grows out of the soil where it is rooted, uncontrolled, uncouth, and wild, uncramped by any of the meannesses of custom. It is 'of the earth, earthy'. It seems almost to have been dug out of the ground, with a soul instinctively superadded to it answering to its wants and origin. Vulgarity is not natural coarseness, but conventional coarseness, learned from others.

From W. HAZLITT, *Characters of Shakespeare's Plays* (1817)

When Shakespeare seems most to recede from humanity he will be found the truest to it. From beyond the scope of Nature if he summon possible existences, he subjugates them to the law of her consistency. He is beautifully loyal to that sovereign directress, even when he appears most to betray and desert her. His ideal tribes submit to policy; his very monsters are tamed to his hand, even as that wild sea-brood, shepherded by Proteus. He tames, and he clothes them with attributes of flesh and blood, till they wonder at themselves, like Indian Islanders forced to submit to European vesture. Caliban, the Witches, are as true to the laws of their own nature (ours with a difference) as Othello, Hamlet, and Macbeth. Herein the great and the little wits are differenced—that if the latter wander ever so little from Nature or actual existence, they lose themselves and their readers. Their phantoms are lawless; their visions nightmares. They do not create, which implies shaping and consistency. Their imaginations are not active, for to be active is to call something into act and form, but passive, as men in sick dreams. For the supernatural, or something superadded to what we know of Nature, they give you the plainly non-natural.

From C. LAMB, *The Sanity of True Genius* (1826).

And, speaking of Caliban, we may note how little attention has been paid to what Shakespeare has emphasized, subtly but unmistakably—his reformation, or, to be more precise, the dawn of morality in his soul. For in one point the gross Caliban is superior to the delicate and charming Ariel: he has a soul, and is therefore capable of moral development, whereas Ariel is but an elemental spirit, without heart, or conscience, or human motives, whose aversion to the earthy and abhorred commands of Sycorax is but the instinctive recoil of opposites. Caliban's father may have been a devil, but his mother was human—and he can be saved. Thus it comes that, at the end of the play, he is like a child who has made his first self-adjustment to the intellectual and moral forces of the world. 'Ay, that I will!' he replies, in hearty obedience to Prospero's command:

> Ay, that I will! and I'll be wise hereafter,
> And seek for grace. . . .

From G. L. KITTREDGE, *Shakespeare* (1916).

APPENDIX I

THE LIFE OF WILLIAM SHAKESPEARE

(condensed from Sir Edmund Chambers's *William Shakespeare*)

WILLIAM SHAKESPEARE was born of middle-class parents at Stratford-on-Avon, a provincial market town of some importance, at an uncertain date between April 24, 1563, and April 23, 1564. His parents were natives of Warwickshire. His father, John Shakespeare, whose principal business was that of glover, rose high in civic life, becoming alderman in 1565 and bailiff in 1568, but later fell on evil days. His mother was Mary Arden. Shakespeare was educated at King Edward VI's Grammar School, Stratford, where he must have learnt a fair amount of Latin, if little or no Greek. He married in 1582 Anne Hathaway, and his first child, a daughter, was baptized in May 1583, to be followed in February 1585 by twins, Hamnet (died 1596) and Judith, who survived her father.

We have no certain information as to Shakespeare's life between 1584 and 1592. There is an early tradition that he stole deer from Sir T. Lucy of Charlecote. We know Shakespeare was in London by 1592 but not when he went there. During these years Shakespeare must have acquired the varied knowledge and experience of life shown in his plays.

The mention of Shakespeare in a death-bed letter of the playwright Greene in September 1592, shows that as a writer for the stage Shakespeare was just becoming a serious rival to the university wits—Marlowe, Peele, Nashe, and Lodge. The years when the theatres were closed on account of plague gave time for the poems *Venus and Adonis* (1593) and *Lucrece* (1594), both dedicated to the Earl of Southampton. By March 1595 Shakespeare was a shareholder in the acting company of the Lord Chamberlain's men, who divided with the Admiral's men the command of the London stage from about 1594 to 1603. For this company, which later became the King's men, Shakespeare seems to have written during the rest of his career. After 1599 most of his plays were performed at the Globe Theatre.

Shakespeare probably wrote his *Sonnets* between 1595 and 1600, but they were not printed till 1609.

In 1596 Shakespeare obtained a grant of arms; in 1597 he bought New Place, a substantial house and garden at Stratford, but he is still found living in London in 1597, 1599, and 1604. Shakespeare occasionally appeared as an actor himself, chiefly before 1598.

About 1610 Shakespeare retired to Stratford, and he wrote no more after 1613. He took no part in civic life, and died on 23 April 1616. There is no reason to reject the report that he died of fever contracted from drinking too hard at a merry meeting with Drayton and Ben Jonson. The family is extinct.

TABLE OF APPROXIMATE DATES OF SHAKESPEARE'S PLAYS

1590–1.
   2 Henry VI.
   3 Henry VI.

1591–2.
   1 Henry VI.

1592–3.
   Richard III.
   Comedy of Errors.

1593–4.
   Titus Andronicus.
   Taming of the Shrew.

1594–5.
   Two Gentlemen of Verona.
   Love's Labour's Lost.
   Romeo and Juliet.

1595–6.
   Richard II.
   Midsummer-Night's Dream.

1596–7.
   King John.
   Merchant of Venice.

1597–8.
   1 Henry IV.
   2 Henry IV.

1598–9.
   Much Ado About Nothing.
   Henry V.

1599–1600.
   Julius Caesar.
   As You Like It.
   Twelfth Night.

1600–1.
   Hamlet.
   Merry Wives of Windsor.

1601–2.
   Troilus and Cressida.

1602–3.
  All's Well That Ends Well.

1603–4.
  ————

1604–5.
  Measure for Measure.
  Othello.

1605–6.
  King Lear.
  Macbeth.

1606–7.
  Antony and Cleopatra.

1607–8.
  Coriolanus.
  Timon of Athens.

1608–9.
  Pericles.

1609–10.
  Cymbeline.

1610–11.
  Winter's Tale.

1611–12.
  Tempest.

1612–13.
  Henry VIII.
  Two Noble Kinsmen.

APPENDIX II

A NOTE ON SHAKESPEARE'S LANGUAGE

By C. T. ONIONS

VOCABULARY. As the *Oxford Shakespeare Glossary* shows, there are some ten thousand words in the whole of the works attributed to Shakespeare which require explanation for the general reader, either because they are no longer in ordinary use or because they are used by him in some way that is not now familiar. Among the former are such words as *ballow* cudgel, *phill-horse* shaft-horse, and *neaf* fist, which are now only provincial, and such others as *benison* blessing, *foison* abundance, *mow* grimace, *parlous* dangerous, *puissant* powerful, *teen* grief, which may be found still in literary diction, as well as a considerable number that have been used, so far as we know, by Shakespeare alone. With such as these we become acquainted by reference to glossaries and notes. But it is possible to continue to read Shakespeare without properly understanding him because we are unaware of, and sometimes do not even suspect, differences in the meaning of words that are in general use to-day. The following selection of such words will serve to indicate the nature of the differences that may be looked for:

allow approve

argument proof, subject of discourse

brave fine, splendid

churchman clergyman

close secret

complexion habit or constitution of body or mind, look, aspect, appearance

conceit idea, thought, invention

condition covenant, rank, character

difference disagreement, dispute

evil disease

fashion sort

favour appearance, face

feature bodily form

gear affair, business

grudge complain

hint opportunity

hope expect, suppose

infer allege

instance cause, evidence, proof

level aim

lewd bad, vile

liberal unrestrained, licentious

mere absolute, downright

merely entirely

miss do without

note sign, stigma, information

obsequious dutiful

owe own

painful laborious

passion painful disease, strong emotion

peevish silly, perverse

present immediate

presently at once

prevent anticipate

quality rank, profession

rate estimation

respect consideration

sad grave, serious

shrewd mischievous, bad

sort rank, class, way, manner

still always, continually

stomach inclination, angry or proud temper

sudden swift, violent

tall fine, valiant

type mark, badge

very true, complete

Among words having a very wide range of meaning the following may be noted:

humour (1) moisture, (2) any of the four fluids of the human body recognized by the old physiologists, (3) temperament, (4) mood, temper, fancy, caprice, inclination;

nice (1) delicate, (2) shy, coy, (3) fastidious, (4) subtle,

minute, (5) trivial, (6) critical, precarious, (7) exact,
precise;

quaint (1) skilled, clever, (2) pretty, dainty, (3) handsome,
elegant, (4) carefully elaborated;

sensible (1) sensitive, (2) of the senses, (3) capable of emotion, (4) rational, (5) tangible, substantial, (6) full of good
sense;

wit (1) mental powers, mind, faculty of perception, as in *the
five wits*, (2) inventive power, (3) understanding, intelligence, (4) wisdom, good sense, as in *brevity is the soul of
wit*, (5) lively fancy producing brilliant talk.

A second adjective **dear** grievous, severe, dire (distinct from
dear beloved, precious) is seen in *my dear offence, thy dear exile*.

Many adjectives and participial words show the application
of a suffix with a force different from that which is now usual:

deceivable deceitful	**questionable** inviting question
tuneable tuneful	**careless** uncared for
unmeritable undeserving	**unexpressive** inexpressible
cureless incurable	**plausive** plausible
grac'd gracious	**unavoided** inevitable
guiled treacherous	**beholding** obliged, beholden
disdain'd disdainful	**timeless** untimely, premature

Note also the double meaning, active and passive, of **artificial** (1) constructive, creative, (2) produced by art.

Shakespeare uses a multitude of technical terms of the arts
and sciences; these are treated in their historical setting in
Shakespeare's England (O.U.P.); note especially the glossary of
musical terms in vol. ii, pp. 32 ff. Some general aspects of the
vocabulary are dealt with in G. S. Gordon's *Shakespeare's
English*, Society for Pure English, Tract xxix (O.U.P.).

PRONUNCIATION. In order to understand the scansion
of the verse it is necessary to bear in mind certain features of
the pronunciation of the time. Many words of French or Latin
origin had been variously stressed from early times, and devia-
tion from present usage is to be seen, for example, in Shakespeare's *adver'tizèd, aspect', canon'izèd, chas'tise, compact'*

(noun), *exile'*, *instinct'* (noun), *obdu'rate*, *reven'ue*, *sepul'chre*, *solem'nizéd*, *triumph'ing*. The stressing of certain adjectives and participles of two syllables is subject to the rule that immediately before nouns of one syllable, and before other nouns stressed on the first syllable, they themselves are stressed on the first syllable, but in other positions on the second; thus: *all' the com'plete ar'mour*, *ev'ery way' complete'*; *the en'tire sum'*, *your' entire' affec'tion*; *the crown' so foul' misplaced'*, *the mis'placed John'*.

In words in *-ian*, *-ience*, *-ient*, *-ion*, these endings may count as two syllables; thus, *Christian*, *patient* may be 3 syllables, *condition*, *impatience* 4, *lamentation* 5. Similarly *marriage* and *soldier* may be three syllables. There is variation in such words as *fire*, *hour*, *power*, *prayer*, which may count as either one or two syllables. *Either* and *neither* may be slurred into one syllable, and *whether* is often so reduced, the form *where* frequently occurring in the old editions, continuing what was a regular early English variant form. *Hither*, *thither*, *whither*, and *having*, *evil*, *devil* are treated in the same way. *Statue* occurs in several passages in the old editions where three syllables are required; many modern editions substitute *statua*, which was a common Tudor and Stuart form.

NOUNS. The genitive singular ending *s* may be replaced by *his*, as *the count* **his** *galleys*, *Mars* **his** *armour*. The inflexion is dropped before *sake*, e.g. *for justice sake*, *for heaven sake*. Proper names often occur without inflexion, where the genitive might be expected, or *of*: e.g. *Venice gold*, *Rome gates*, *Tiber banks*. One of the adverbial uses of the genitive is preserved in *come your ways*. Notable examples of the *n*-plural are *shoon* for *shoes*, and *eyne* (eyes), which are used chiefly for rhyme. *Aches* is of two syllables, since the noun *ache* was pronounced *aitch*, as distinct from the verb, which was regularly spelt *ake* in the old editions. Names of measures and periods of time are often uninflected, as *twelve year*, *a thousand pound*: cf. *sennight* (= seven nights) week.

ADJECTIVES. Adjectives are converted into nouns with greater freedom than at present: *fair* is used for beauty as well as for lady, *the general* for the public, the multitude, *the subject* for the people of a state. Note the phrases: *in few* in few words, in short; *by small and small* little by little; *the most* (= majority) *of men. Enow* represents the old plural of *enough*, and is so used, always following its noun or pronoun. *Mo, moe* (= more) is also plural: it represents an old comparative adverb, which was used at first with a genitive, but became in time an adjective like *more*. The plural of *other* is either *others* or *other* (e.g. *and then come in the other*).

Peculiarities in the comparison of adjectives are: the use of the suffixes where we prefer *more* and *most*, as *certainer, perfecter, violentest*; the addition of *-er* to a comparative, as *worser*; the use of *more* and *most* with comparatives and superlatives, as *more better, most best, most dearest, more worthier, most worst, most unkindest*. Note the old comparative *near*, as in *ne'er the near*. An absolute superlative may be strengthened by prefixing *one*, e.g. *one the truest-mannered*.

PRONOUNS. The distinction between the familiar or contemptuous *thou* (*thee, thy*) and the respectful *ye* (*you, your*) is in general preserved. The old weak form *a* of *he* occurs in *There was a gaming*. The commonest genitive of *it* is *his*; the present-day *its* and the obsolete *it* (as in *It had* it *head bit off by* it *young*) are about equally frequent in the old editions. Pronominal possessive forms are sometimes used as adjectives, but only in company with other possessives, as in *his and* mine *lov'd darling*. Note the position of the possessive in *good* my *liege, sweet* my *coz*.

There is much irregularity in the use of the cases of pronouns. *Thee* is used for *thou*, as with intransitive imperatives, *look thee, stand thee close*; also in *I would not be thee*, and the like. We find also: *between you and* I*; Is she as tall as* me*?; Which, of* he *or Adrian . . . ?; Damn'd* be him *. . .* The functions of the original nominative *ye* and objective *you* are reversed in *I do beseech* ye*, if* you *bear me hard . . .; us* is usual for *we* in the interrogative *Shall*'s. There is no consistency in the use of *who* and *whom*; a common confusion is illustrated in whom *they say is killed*.

The relative pronouns are not discriminated according to present practice, since *which* may refer to persons and *who* to things. *The which* is very frequent; it may be used adjectivally, as in *For the which blessing I am at him upon my knees*. The nominative relative (the subject of the clause) is often absent, as in *There be some sports are painful.* After a negative or an interrogative, *but* is frequently used as a relative = that . . . not; e.g. *No man* but *prophesied revenge for it; What canst thou say* but *will perplex them more?*

VERBS. Verbs show many old forms as well as a variety of conjugation which are no longer possible in ordinary language.

Early strong forms are retained in *holp, holp'st,* alongside *helped, helped'st; spake* and *spoke* are both in use; old strong forms are replaced by weak in *becomed, shaked;* the past tenses *drunk* and *sprung* are more frequent than *drank* and *sprang;* the clipped *broke, spoke* occur beside the original participial forms *broken, spoken; catched* and *caught* are both found; many past tense forms are used for the past participle, as *eat, holp, forsook, rode, shook, swam.* Remarkable instances of the great variety of usage may be seen in *struck, strucken, stricken,* for the past participle of *strike,* and in the conjugation *write,* past tense *writ,* occasionally *wrote,* past participle *written, writ,* less frequently *wrote.* Weak verbs of which the stem ends in *d* or *t* often have shortened past participles, as *betid, heat, wed, wet.* Observe that *graft* and *hoist* are rather participles of the older verbs *graff* and *hoise* than of *graft* and *hoist.*

Present tense forms in *s* (including *is*) are not uncommonly used with plural subjects, especially where the verb precedes the subject; e.g. *What cares these roarers for the name of king?; There is no more such masters.*

There are many survivals of impersonal uses, some of them in disguise. The older forms of *I were better, Thou'rt best* were *Me were better* It would be better for me, *Thee were best* It would be best for thee; but in *You were better* the case of the pronoun became ambiguous, *you* was in time felt as a nominative, and other pronouns fell into line. The history of the development of *I am woe* (in which *woe* is felt as an adjective) from the original *Me is woe* is somewhat similar. In *Fair befall thee* the verb is impersonal and *fair* an adverb.

The uses of the subjunctive are many and various. An exceptional construction is seen in **Live** *thou* (= if thou live), *I live.* An old use of the past subjunctive is exemplified in *If you would put me to verses, Kate, why, you* **undid** (= would undo) *me.*

The infinitive of a verb of motion is often to be supplied in thought with an auxiliary verb; e.g. *I must to England;* **Shall** *we to this gear?*

ADVERBS. Adverbs, especially those of one syllable, may have the same form as their corresponding adjectives, as *dear, full, fair, near, true*; such words as *excellent, equal, instant, prodigal* are also used adverbially. When two adverbs are coupled together which would both normally have the suffix *-ly*, one of them may lack it, as in *sprightfully and bold, so lamely and unfashionable.* A rare formation is *chirurgeonly* like a surgeon. Comparative forms with the suffix are used more freely than at present; e.g. *earth*lier *happy, wise*lier.

The use of *but* in the sense of 'only' needs to be specially noticed: *but now* just now, only this moment; similarly *but while-ere* only a short time ago, *but late* only lately. It is coupled redundantly with *only* in *He only lived but till he was a man.*

Normally, *only* should stand immediately before the words it modifies; but it is often loosely placed, as in *He only loves the world for him* (i.e. only for him).

A negative adverb (or conjunction) may be used with another negative word, superfluously from our point of view (the use was originally emphatic): *You know my father hath no child but I,* **nor none** *is like to have.* The negative may even be tripled: *Love no man in good earnest;* **nor no** *further in sport* **neither.** In the following a redundant negative occurs in a dependent clause after a verb of negative meaning: *You may deny that you were* **not** *the cause.*

PREPOSITIONS. Prepositions have many uses that differ from their present ones; for example, *for, of,* and *to* have each some ten meanings that are not current now. *Of* and *with* are both used to express the agent, as in *seen* **of** *us, torn to pieces* **with** *a bear,* or the instrument, as in *provided* **of** *a torch-bearer, killed* **with** *a thunderstroke.* With abstract nouns, *of* forms equivalents of the corresponding adjectives; e.g. *of desperation* desperate, *of nature* natural. Both *for* and *to* may be used, though in different kinds of context, = in the character of, as: e.g. *turned out of all towns and cities* **for** *a dangerous thing; I have a king here* **to** *my flatterer.* A preposition is used freely at the end of the sentence or clause, e.g. *he I am before* = he in whose presence I am; sometimes it is redundant, as in *the scene wherein we play in*; or again, it may be dropped, as in *I see thou lovest me not with the full weight that I love thee* (i.e. *with*).

At in *at door*, *at gate*, and the like, is descended from the earlier *atte* (two syllables), which is for *at the*.

CONJUNCTIONS. The following should be noted: *an* or *an if* if; *as* as if; *for* because; *but* if . . . not, unless; *nor . . nor . .* neither *. . nor . .*, *or . . or . .* either *. . or . .*; *or ere* before ever; *so* provided that; *that* (in much wider use than at present) for the reason that, because, in order that, so that; *whiles* while.

The full exposition of the language of Shakespeare requires a book to itself, and such will be found in E. A. Abbott's *Shakespearian Grammar* and W. Franz's *Shakespeare-Grammatik*. An illuminating sketch is Henry Bradley's essay 'Shakespeare's English' in *Shakespeare's England*, vol. ii, pp. 539–74. Selected points are treated with some fullness in *Nine Plays of Shakespeare* (O.U.P.), pp. xix–xxxvi.

APPENDIX III

A NOTE ON METRE

SHAKESPEARE'S plays are written, for the most part, in blank (i.e. unrhymed) verse with a varying proportion of prose and an occasional song in lyric metres in some plays. In *The Tempest* prose is used for the lower characters (e.g. Stephano, Trinculo), and verse for those of nobler rank (e.g. Prospero, Alonso, Ferdinand, Miranda). There are, however, exceptions. The boatswain, for instance, who speaks in prose in I. i, rises to verse in V. i, perhaps because he is talking seriously and respectfully to his king, and not bawling orders to the crew. In II. i the wit combat of Antonio and Sebastian with Gonzalo is carried on (as is natural) in prose, though elsewhere those characters express themselves in blank verse. That Ariel always speaks in verse is in keeping with his poetical nature; and Caliban, the natural savage, is distinguished from the vulgar products of civilization by his tendency to speak in verse, or in rhythmical prose. The mythical characters of the Masque—Juno, Ceres, Iris—talk in rhymed verse, in accordance with an established tradition of the Jacobean masque.

Blank verse had been in use on the Elizabethan stage for a generation, and about 1590 Christopher Marlowe had brought it to perfection in his 'mighty line'. Although all unrhymed verse might be called 'blank verse', the name is specially applied to the line consisting *normally* of ten syllables with five stresses or accents. It is common to use the terminology of classical verse and, if we understand that a long syllable in Latin or Greek corresponds to an accented or 'more conspicuous' syllable in English, we may describe blank verse as five iambic feet (i.e. five feet each consisting of an iambus, scanning ∪ –). But whereas in classical verse quantity was rigid and the variations allowed from the pattern were strictly limited, in English verse very few lines conform absolutely to the pattern by having an equally strong accent on five of ten syllables. In Shakespeare not only is the accent either altogether absent, or reversed (– ∪ for ∪ –), in some feet, but often we have more, and occasionally fewer, than ten syllables in a line. A poet can make almost any departure from the norm, provided he does not destroy the sense of that pattern underlying his verse in the reader's mind. It is essential for all readers of Shakespeare first to acquire a consciousness of the pattern, and for this purpose they may scan lines by stressing the syllables that should bear an accent, thus:

∪   –   ∪   –   ∪   –   ∪   –   ∪   –
As wic|ked dew | as e'er | my mot|her brush'd . . .

(I. ii. 321.)

The sense of this line in its context allows us to read it with some stress on all the syllables marked long and accented, but this is quite the exception. The other extreme is seen in the line 'Íf by | your árt, | my deárest | fáther, | you háve' (I. ii. 1), which must be pronounced as here marked, and *not*, as the pattern would suggest, 'If bý | your árt, | my deár | est fáth | er, you háve.'

As Shakespeare grew older his metrical practice underwent considerable modification. Speaking generally, it may be said that in his early plays he shows a fondness for rhyme; his blank verse, though very far from rigid, does not often depart widely from the regular pattern, either in the number of syllables, or in the distribution of the stresses; and there is a natural pause, as often as not, at the end of a line. In his latest plays there is little rhyme; the blank verse is extremely irregular, and follows far more closely the natural rhythms of speech; and the sense is far more frequently carried over from one line to the next. Shakespeare's metrical practice develops so steadily in these various respects that 'verse tests' have been used to help in dating his plays. The increased metrical freedom of his later plays is perhaps most easily recognized in his fondness for double, or 'feminine', endings to a blank-verse line, as in 'Now in the waist, the deck, in every cabin' (I. ii. 197, and see the whole of Ariel's speech, ll. 195–206). Except for the purposes of learning the pattern, we should always read by the sense and leave the metre to take care of itself. (For a brief treatment of Shakespeare's variations such as extra syllables, 'weak endings', &c. see Dowden's *Shakespeare Primer*, pp. 39, &c., and for a more general view of the subject, E. Hamer: *The Metres of English Poetry*.)

APPENDIX IV

A. Extract from *A Discovery of the Barmudas, Otherwise called the Ile of Divels*, by Silvester Jourdan, 1610.

I being in ship called the Sea-venture, with Sir Thomas Gates, Sir George Somers, and Captaine Newport . . bound for Virginia, in the height of thirty degrees of northerly latitude, or thereabouts: we were taken with a most sharpe and cruell storme upon the five and twentieth day of July, Anno 1609, which did separate us from the residue of our fleete, (which were eight in number). . . .

[The sailors are driven almost to despair by the violence of the storm]. . . . So that some of them having some good and comfortable waters in the ship, fetcht them, and drunke one to the other, taking their last leave one of the other, untill their more ioyfull and happy meeting, in a more blessed world; when it pleased God out of his most gracious and mercifull providence, so to direct and guide our ship (being left to the mercy of the sea) for her most advantage, that Sir George Somers (sitting upon the poope of the ship) . . . most wishedly happily discryed

land. . . . And the ship kept from present sinking, . . . it pleased
God to send her within halfe an English mile of that land that
Sir George Somers had not long before discryed: which were the
Ilandes of the Barmudas. And there neither did our ship sincke,
but more fortunately in so great a misfortune, fell in betweene
two rockes, where she was fast lodged and locked, for further
budging. . . .

For the Ilandes of the Barmudas, as every man knoweth that
hath heard or read of them, were never inhabited by any Christian or Heathen people, but ever esteemed, and reputed, a most
prodigious and inchanted place, affoording nothing but gusts,
stormes, and foule weather; which made every Navigator and
Mariner to avoide them. . . . Yet did we finde there the ayre so
temperate and the Country so abundantly fruitful of all fit
necessaries, for the sustentation and preservation of mans life,
that . . . we were there for the space of nine moneths (few dayes
over or under) . . . well refreshed. . . .

Another Sea fowle there is that lyeth in little holes in the
ground, like unto a cony-hole, and are in great numbers, ex-
ceeding good meate. . . . There are also great store and plenty
of Herons, and those so familiar and tame, that wee beate them
downe from the trees with stones and staves.

B. Extract from *A true reportory of the wracke and re-
    demption of Sir Thomas Gates, Knight*. By William
    Strachey, dated 15th July, 1610.

On S. James his day, July 24, being Monday (preparing for
no less all the blacke night before) the cloudes gathering thicke
upon us, and the windes singing, and whistling most unusually,
which made us to cast off our Pinnace towing the same untill
then asterne, a dreadfull storme and hideous began to blow
from out the North-east, which swelling, and roaring as it were
by fits, some houres with more violence than others, at length
did beate all light from heaven; which like an hell of darknesse
turned blacke upon us, so much the more fuller of horror. . . .
Our clamours dround in the windes, and the windes in thunder.
Prayers might well be in the heart and lips, but drowned in the
outcries of the Officers: nothing heard that could give confort,
nothing seene that might incourage hope. . . .

During all this time, the heavens look'd so blacke upon us, that it was not possible the elevation of the Pole might be observed: nor a Starre by night, nor Sunne beame by day was to be seene. Onely upon the thursday night Sir George Summers being upon the watch, had an apparition of a little round light, like a faint Starre, trembling, and streaming along with a sparkeling blaze, halfe the height upon the Maine Mast, and shooting sometimes from Shroud to Shroud, tempting to settle as it were upon any of the foure Shrouds: and for three or foure houres together, or rather more, halfe the night it kept with us; running sometimes along the Maine-yard to the very end, and then returning. . . . The Italians, and such, who lye open to the Adriatique and Tyrrene Sea, call it (a sacred body) Corpo sancto: the Spaniards call it Saint Elmo. . . .

[They sight land, and manage to run their ship aground, bringing off 'men, women, and children, about the number of one hundred and fifty, safe into the Iland'. They find that they are among the Bermudas.]

They are full of Shawes of goodly Cedar, fairer than ours here of Virginia: the Berries whereof our men seething, straining, and letting stand some three or foure daies, made a kind of pleasant drinke. . . . Sure it is that there are no Rivers nor running Springs of fresh water to be found upon any of them: when wee came first wee digged and found certaine gushings and soft bublings. . . . According as their raines fell, we had our Wels and Pits (which we digged). . . .

Fowle there is in great store. . . . A kinde of webbe-footed Fowle there is, of the bignesse of an English green Plover, or Sea-Meawe, which all the Summer wee saw not, and in the darkest nights of November and December (for in the night they onely feed) they would come forth, but not flye far from home, and hovering in the ayre, and over the Sea, made a strange hollow and harsh howling . . . and there in the ground they have their Burrowes, like Conyes in a Warren, . . . which Birds with a light bough in a darke night (as in our Lowbelling[1]) wee caught . . . which Birds for their blindnesse (for they see weakly in the day) and for their crying and whooting, wee called the Sea Owle.

[[1] In fowling, a bell ('lowbell') was often used to frighten the birds, When so terrified, the birds were easily netted.]

APPENDIX V

Extract from *Caliban upon Setebos*; *Or, Natural Theology in the Island*, by Robert Browning.

[IN this poem (which extends to 295 lines) Browning imagines Caliban lying on a hot summer day in his cave, puzzling his brain about the nature of God—'my dam's God, Setebos'. Browning's Caliban may not be Shakespeare's, but he has the same queer mixture of brutality and poetry, of clumsiness and sensitiveness. Caliban is here made to speak of himself in the third person, but omitting the subject, e.g. '(Caliban) will sprawl' &c.]

'Will sprawl, now that the heat of day is best,
Flat on his belly in the pit's much mire,
With elbows wide, fists clenched to prop his chin;
And, while he kicks both feet in the cool slush,
And feels about his spine small eft-things course,
Run in and out each arm, and make him laugh;
And while above his head a pompion-plant,
Coating the cave-top as a brow its eye,
Creeps down to touch and tickle hair and beard,
And now a flower drops with a bee inside,   10
And now a fruit to snap at, catch and crunch:
He looks out o'er yon sea which sunbeams cross
And recross till they weave a spider-web
(Meshes of fire, some great fish breaks at times),
And talks to his own self, howe'er he please,
Touching that other, whom his dam called God.
Because to talk about Him, vexes—ha,
Could He but know! and time to vex is now,
When talk is safer than in winter-time.
Moreover Prosper and Miranda sleep   20
In confidence he drudges at their task,
And it is good to cheat the pair, and gibe,
Letting the rank tongue blossom into speech.

Setebos, Setebos, and Setebos!
'Thinketh, He dwelleth i' the cold o' the moon.
'Thinketh He made it, with the sun to match,
But not the stars; the stars came otherwise;
Only made clouds, winds, meteors, such as that:
Also this isle, what lives and grows thereon,
And snaky sea which rounds and ends the same.   30

'Thinketh, it came of being ill at ease:
He hated that He cannot change His cold,
Nor cure its ache. 'Hath spied an icy fish
That longed to 'scape the rock-stream where she lived,
And thaw herself within the lukewarm brine
O' the lazy sea her stream thrusts far amid,
A crystal spike 'twixt two warm walls of wave;
Only she ever sickened, found repulse
At the other kind of water, not her life,
(Green-dense and dim-delicious, bred o' the sun)   40
Flounced back from bliss she was not born to breathe,
And in her old bounds buried her despair,
Hating and loving warmth alike: so He.

'Thinketh, He made thereat the sun, this isle,
Trees and the fowls here, beast and creeping thing.
Yon otter, sleek-wet, black, lithe as a leech;
Yon auk, one fire-eye in a ball of foam,
That floats and feeds; a certain badger brown
He hath watched hunt with that slant white-wedge eye
By moonlight; and the pie with the long tongue   50
That pricks deep into oakwarts for a worm,
And says a plain word when she finds her prize.
But will not eat the ants; the ants themselves
That build a wall of seeds and settled stalks
About their hole—He made all these and more,
Made all we see, and us, in spite: how else?
He could not, Himself, make a second self
To be His mate; as well have made Himself.
He would not make what He mislikes or slights,

An eyesore to Him, or not worth His pains: 60
But did, in envy, listlessness or sport,
Make what Himself would fain, in a manner, be—
Weaker in most points, stronger in a few,
Worthy, and yet mere playthings all the while,
Things He admires and mocks too,—that is it.
Because, so brave, so better though they be,
It nothing skills if He begin to plague.
Look now, I melt a gourd-fruit into mash,
Add honeycomb and pods, I have perceived,
Which bite like finches when they bill and kiss,—   70
Then, when froth rises bladdery, drink up all,
Quick, quick, till maggots scamper through my brain;
And throw me on my back i' the seeded thyme,
And wanton, wishing I were born a bird.
Put case, unable to be what I wish,
I yet could make a live bird out of clay:
Would not I take clay, pinch my Caliban
Able to fly?—for, there, see, he hath wings,
And great comb like the hoopoe's to admire,
And there, a sting to do his foes offence,   80
There, and I will that he begin to live,
Fly to yon rock-top, nip me off the horns
Of grigs high up that make the merry din,
Saucy through their veined wings, and mind me not.
In which feat, if his leg snapped, brittle clay,
And he lay stupid-like,—why, I should laugh;
And if he, spying me, should fall to weep,
Beseech me to be good, repair his wrong,
Bid his poor leg smart less or grow again,—
Well, as the chance were, this might take or else   90
Not take my fancy: I might hear his cry,
And give the manikin three legs for his one,
Or pluck the other off, leave him like an egg,
And lessoned he was mine and merely clay.
Were this no pleasure, lying in the thyme,
Drinking the mash, with brain become alive,
Making and marring clay at will? So He.